GROWING DEEP ROOTS

Finding Rest for Your Soul Through
Denying Self, Taking Up Your Cross and
His Yoke, and Learning of Him

ORA MILLER

Taught from childhood to adulthood in the
Amish culture and beliefs

PAGE PUBLISHING, INC.
Conneaut Lake, PA

First originally published by Page Publishing 2020

ISBN 978-1-6624-0563-1 (pbk)
ISBN 978-1-6624-0564-8 (digital)

Printed in the United States of America

I would like to dedicate this book to Orpha Miller, my beloved wife, and our children: Arlene, Ervin, Lloyd, Leona, Elvie, Becky, Lorrie, and Joas; our grandchildren: Abigail and Judith Coblentz (artists; and give a special thanks to Danita Jordan (typist/editing) and Dan Burns (friend/consult).

A few words in regards to how this book became into reality. The first thing that happened is that I spent 25 years plus writing things down as they came to mind. Ninety nine percent was written between 1:00 and 5:00 A.M. This went on until the year 2018. In that year, I worked on getting it together in somewhat of a book fashion. About ⅓ of my writings were included. I made twelve copies and along with these copies was one letter trying to describe what I was asking. I asked them if they had any interest in commenting and helping me to get these writings into a book form basically for my children and the children that might come along later or to throw it in the trash and forget about it. Maybe they would say something like this, you might have something for your grandchildren, however, I am not qualified to help with the matter. Good luck and blessings.

I personally talk a lot about "naysayers". Also, I made a quote something like this, "You cannot depend on naysayers, oftentimes you would be better served if you would do the opposite of their advice".

Nevertheless in regards to these writings, I thought this was over the top. Ten trusted couples received the writings and not a single response. My thinking went something like this, not a single word and not a peep from anyone. This has to be the biggest flop of my life. I might as well take a big swallow and a deep breath and accept it for what it is and go on with my life.

However about a year after this episode came into reality, I was talking to a very good gentleman and a precious friend. As we were visiting, I mentioned something about these writings that I wrote over the years. I explained how after making these writings public to ten trusted people for comment and getting no feedback, I gave up and ditched the whole matter as one of my biggest disappointments of my life.

He then asked me if he could read them. I said, "Sure". So, I gave him somewhere between 25 and 50 pages. A little later, he came to me and said something like this, those writings that you gave me to read, *Forget about all the naysayers!* Humble yourself and print them in a book for whoever wants to read them. If it should help just one person, give god the glory. For that, there is no shame!

Therefore, I am telling everyone who might read this (with his permission) I am stating here that the friend by the name of Dan Burns is the man responsible for getting this book that you hold in your hands into print.

If perhaps he did well, give god the glory and if not, tell us or drop the matter. Another person having a big impact in this book becoming a reality is the daughter of Mr. Burns. Her name is Danita Jordan, she is a wife and a mother and she did all the typing and the first edit and layout of this book. Once a week for roughly thirty weeks Dan, Danita and I came together and put my writings into a book form.

In the meantime, we had information of a publishing company by the name of Page Publishing. We researched their credibility and found them to be a very reputable company. They advised us that they would look at the manuscript, study it and let us know if they would accept it.

As you can see in your hand they accepted it, therefore we signed a contract with them. We have found that the company is all of what we had gathered earlier.

Contents

Introduction 7
Preface 9
Chapter 1:   First Memories 19
Chapter 2:   Thankful for Health 34
Chapter 3:   The People We Meet 44
Chapter 4:   Seventy-Acre Farm 59
Chapter 5:   Everyday Happenings 67
Chapter 6:   Hunting and Fishing 81
Chapter 7:   Business Challenges 97
Chapter 8:   Missionary Service 117
Chapter 9:   Libby Happenings 122
Chapter 10: Orpha and I, Beginning 136
Chapter 11: Commitment for Life 145
Chapter 12: Teaching and Believing 167

INTRODUCTION

Our Relationship with God

"Behold the fowls of the air… Consider the lilies of the field." Matt. 6:26–28

Why should we consider the lilies? Isn't it just simply because they are? They don't do great wonders and works. Yet, they fulfill a useful purpose by their beauty. We also shouldn't be concerned about our usefulness. Our only concern should be our relationship with God. Get rightly related to him, and he will let us bloom without us knowing it. Not that we will now stand out as somebody—far from it—yet rivers of living water will flow out of you.

Here again the concentration is not on ourselves but on God. Our circumstances are well known by our father in heaven. How we grow spiritually, like the lilies, is in direct relationship to our relationship with our father in heaven.

If we expect to be of any use to God, we have to become rightly related to Him. Only then can he use us, not our usefulness and not what we do for him. The only thing that counts is his work in us.

PREFACE

It is my hope and prayer that the stories and lessons in the following writings will be accepted as they are meant. The stories are not only entertaining and enlightening but the lessons learned as the events occurred are a reminder of the spiritual opportunities that avail themselves daily throughout our lives. These lines are not to be critical or condemning but much more as an enlightenment to where churches stand today and comparing it to the word of God that he wants us to know.

The carnal nature of man is so bent on doing his own thing, figuring things out through his own thinking, and organizing and planning with his own limited knowledge and understanding it leads to the extent of forming and conforming to certain men's creeds and standards.

During the adventures as a young man and into adulthood, I have been open-minded to learning the way the Holy Spirit, through the word of the Bible, wants us to follow Him. So have fun reading the happenings of my life and the great lessons while remembering to always educate your mind with the true Word and swell your heart in all good things pleasing to the Lord.

"To God Be The Glory!"

DAD AND MOM

Thank You

- For moving to MT, against all odds
- For raising me right, + pouring out of yourselves for me.
- For desiring to give me the best of what you could.
- For loving me + raising me in a functional family.
- For being my DAD + Mom!

Love,
Joas

Mom and Dad,

If it wasn't for your spirit of the pioneer, none of us would be here. Thank you for bringing this rowdy 5 year old along on the first exploration trip to Montana in June 1975. It changed my life forever. You are both my heroes and I'm forever grateful.

Your son Elvis

DEAR
DAD and   ♡ ♡ ♡ ♡
    Mom,
I honor the seed of the Lord that
He planted in you. It took root so that
your children and grandchildren could
also find and follow Him. I bless
    you for being obedient to the
    Lord. I am thankful to be
    a partaker of that. Thank-you
    that you love and care for
    us. I bless you and
        love you in return!
        Because of Jesus...
            dau.
                Becky

From the pioneering years at West Kootenai when many gave up, you didn't.

When hardships of provision and shelter were slim, you stayed the course.

When others turned against you, your song never died.

When your field was taken away you plowed new ground.

When a door closed in front of you you walked through another.

When life gave us lemons, you made lemonade. As youth at home, when we needed to travel or needing a gun to hunt, that came first.

You never controled our choice of lake to fish, forest to hunt, mountain to camp. You blessed our life partners and you chose to stay young. Thank You Lloyd

Dad and Mom,

Adversities, and unfortunate circumstances, financial crisis, physical, emotional and spiritual struggles and challenges, and times of sorrow have been woven into the very threads of your lives and life has not always dealt kindly with thee. But thou rose up and together you have journeyed through these 85 years, approaching the sunset...

Dad, in front of the little mirror of the medicine cabinet, face lathered in shaving cream, razor in hand, singing "Some glad morning when this life is o'er, I'll fly away".

Mom, on her way across the yard, picking up a stick here, a pine cone there. One pine cone at a time makes a difference.   - May the Lord be with thee, - - A heart full of love and a tear in mine eye, Arlene

...written early morn. of Mary Etta's funeral

A tribute to Mom & Dad —   Dec 30, 2011

    I honor the legacy you built and are
leaving for me and us as a family. In your
80+ years you have plowed much ground. Your
pioneering spirit opened the way for generations
to follow and run with your vision. Changes...
they were never easy but you bravely continued —
quitting was never an option for both of you.
    I was blest to live at home for many
years and now to live close by. This is an
opportunity very few experience + to say I am richly
blessed is an under statement.
As I grow older I appreciate
our rich heritage more
and more, and all you
have taught me through living it out. I love you!
            The 6th child... —Leona

ORA MILLER

"Thank-You, Dad & Mom, for helping to make this possible!"

KOOTENAI LOG HOMES
5388 W. Kootenai
Rexford, MT 59930

PURCHASER'S RECEIPT - RETAIN FOR YOUR RECORDS

First National Bank in Libby

49376

93-285-921

REMITTER

Ora and Lloyd Miller

7/01 92

NOT NEGOTIABLE

PAYABLE TO

99,661.45

MEMORANDUM

CASHIER'S CHECK

FOR

16

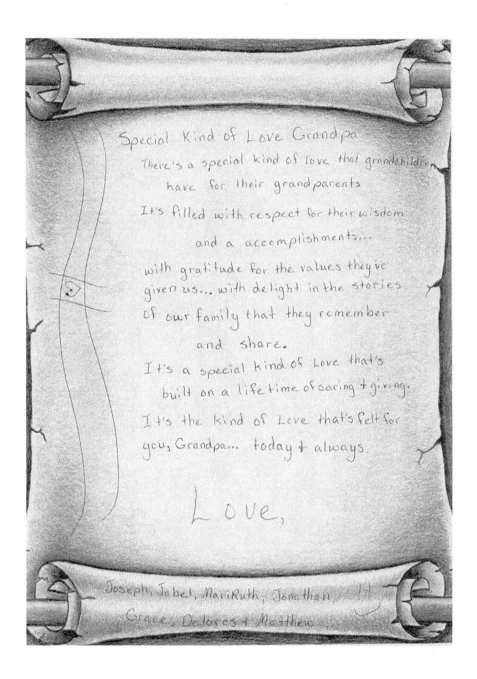

Special Kind of Love Grandpa

There's a special kind of love that grandchildren
have for their grandparents

It's filled with respect for their wisdom

and a accomplishments...

with gratitude for the values they've
given us... with delight in the stories
of our family that they remember
and share.

It's a special kind of Love that's
built on a lifetime of caring + giving.

It's the kind of Love that's felt for
you, Grandpa... today + always.

Love,

Joseph, Jabel, MariRuth, Jonathan,
Grace, Delores + Matthew

Goin' Fishin

CHAPTER 1

First Memories

Family History

In the year 1906 my grandparent, along with his parents, moved to Oklahoma. My dad was one year old and thus far the only child of the young couple. The couple's names were Ananias and his young wife, Mattie (Hershburger) Miller.

There they lived close to the Indians. I am assuming the Indians still lived in teepees, yet I have nothing to back this up. Everyone was trying to keep food on the table. Keeping close contact with the white people helped the Indians. We all know that all livestock die sometimes, and when they lost as much as a chicken or cat, the Indians wanted to know about it. A horse was a great gift.

This went on for ten years before they decided to move back to Indiana. They had saved enough cash for train tickets and rode the train back. They still had the clothes on their backs and in this time had managed to accumulate four more children.

The Muck Farm

This is basically what happened. He had lived in an area where there was an eighty-acre farm for sale. One day the owner came to my grandad and told him he would like to sell him the eighty-acre farm.

Grandad replied, "How could I buy your farm? I have no money."

"You don't have to have money. We'll do it with a hand-shake, only we will put the handshake agreement on paper to clarify what we agreed upon," replied the seller.

Grandad must have tipped his hat a little and scratched his head, thinking, *How would such a deal work out?* Nevertheless, he made the deal, and they shook hands.

Now, the real challenge was in front of him and on his mind, yet how could he turn such an offer down? He knew, where there is a will, there is a way.

The first thing he had to face was his wife. He had to tell her what he did. This was the biggest undertaking since he mustered up enough nerve to ask her if she would marry him.

To this day, or at least in my younger years, this place was always referred to as the muck farm. Muck is decaying matter formed over many, many years. It was good for raising spearmint and peppermint. Mint-farming was rather new in those days, yet as they found more and more uses for mint, the demand was on the upswing. Wrigley's chewing gum became popular at that time.

My grandad started to farm in earnest. He had some boys that could drive horses and helped out in many ways. The mint prices were rising, and things were looking up.

He bought the muck farm with a handshake-agreement down payment one of the first years coming back from Oklahoma.

After a year or two, a neighbor down the road kept hounding him to sell his muck farm to him. Grandad would always say, "It is not for sale!" This went on for another year or so. This neighbor even bugged him when they met in town.

The man asked, "What would you take for your farm today?"

Again, Grandad replied, "Why would I have to tell you again, as I have told you many times, our farm is *not for sale!*"

"Well," the man said, "you would surely at least put a price on the farm?"

"Sure, I could put a price on it," Grandad said. "That price would be so high you'd be out of your mind to take the offer."

The man insisted, "Well, okay. What is that offer?"

"It would have to be twice the price I paid. You can call me whatever you want for asking such a price, but I'm not giving in or taking a penny less."

"I'll take it!" the man said as he handed over ten $100.00 bills for Grandad to hold it. "I'll pay the balance after I go to the bank."

This neighbor had been carrying these bills in his billfold for a number of years, just waiting for the moment that he could catch Grandad in the right mode to sell.

Now Grandad had to go home and break the news to grandma. This was even harder than when he told her he bought it, but looking at the green cash in his hands convinced her it was for real. So she might as well take it in stride. She thought, *'Now what next?'*

Since Grandad had cash in hand, it can be assumed that he could make things happen.

Dilapidated Farm

The Dilapidated Farm

After he sold the muck farm for cash to his neighbor that had been bugging him to sell it to him, he now had cash in his hand to buy the "worthless farm that he thought it was."

I do not know how everything came about, but there was a ditch dug that started at the south end of the property and ran along the east side of the property then turned left to the north end and ran west. The same ditch went along the farm where Orpha, my wife, and I lived for the first two years of our marriage.

Grandad was now living on the land that he earlier had said a person had to be out of his mind to buy it.

In Indiana Grandad went with his uncle Emanuel Miller doing carpentry work. While going to and from work, they went by an unkept farm that grew mostly weeds. What buildings there were, were merely dilapidated shacks.

One day my grandad remarked as they drove by, "Whoever buys this dump would have to be out of his mind." He said this as he looked at the for-sale sign sticking out of the weeds and trash.

His thoughts changed since he now had cash in his hands from selling the muck farm. They had the money to buy the farm, plus extra money to improve the so-called worthless farm, making it into a productive and undilapidated farm for his wife and children. This my grandad did by draining the marsh and building a three-tub mint still, etc.

Well, all of us at times make remarks that come back to bite us. Later on, my grandad realized he had classified himself to be exactly that person. He became the one to purchase this so-called worthless piece of property.

Since the ditch was dug, the land could be farmed. My dad told us boys how they had a sod plow with a long moldboard to break up the sod so they could plant mint. He not only distilled his own mint with his triple tub mint still but people came from far and wide to have him distill their mint too.

They had three crews and ran the still around the clock. Even so, there were wagons lined up to my father-in-law's cross-road that was half a mile down the road. People would sleep on their loads of mint to save their place in line to get their mint distilled. To make sure the line kept moving, the steam whistle was blown each time a tub was empty. At least the ones closest would hear it, wake up, and move forward.

On this farm lives the fourth generation and has hardly any resemblance of the looks of the farm that he bought with the money from the muck farm.

Mint Prices

I am sure most of you have heard the phrase, "Making a mint." Even the government in making-money calls it "a mint." Even though there is no mint involved. They must have gotten it from the farmers that paid their farms off in record time, saying they made "a mint" by farming mint.

Even though many did very well with mint for a number of years, like everything else, everything that goes up must come down, even the price of mint oil. The top known price was around $29.00 dollars per pound. With a price even much less, a person could pay his farm mortgage off in a year or two.

I heard my grandad say two farmers were discussing when the best time might be to sell their mint oil that they were storing in their basements while the prices were ever going up.

One farmer says, "I believe I'll sell mine now. The price they offered me was $25.00 per pound."

"That's an awful good price, and I'm going to sell."

The other farmer said, "It's been going up for a long time." Therefore he said he is going to wait until it gets to $30.00 per pound.

Well, it came close, then it started to drop and drop fast. By the time he was ready to sell, it was down to $20.00 per pound. Therefore, he lost $5.00 per pound if he would have sold it when his neighbor did.

In my time, when my dad raised mint, I do not recall ever getting more than $5.00 per pound. I do remember our dad told us boys if we get a barrel of oil, fifty-five gallons, he will buy us a BB gun.

Therefore, we put every inch, every ounce of energy that we could muster into the mint-farming, helping to fill the barrel.

We put an order in to Montgomery Ward for a one-thousand-shot Daisy Red Ryder BB Gun, only to have the money returned with this note: "We are sorry. We are out of stock at present and do not know when we will get more." This was after the war, yet things were still hard to get.

Nevertheless, over time we got our BB gun. When these guns first came out, a lot of boys had BB guns. Just like some other things, they were still dangerous. Several boys that we knew got BBs in their eye and lost an eye.

Yours truly came really close through my carelessness. I shot at a target about 'thirty or 'forty feet away, and the BB came straight back and lodged between my nose and my eye. Missed my eyeball by about an inch or less.

That taught me a lesson I'll never forget. To this day I cannot shoot a BB gun without thinking of that before I pull the trigger.

Connecting with the Opposite Gender

Growing up in Indiana in a large Amish community, where each church district consisted of approximately thirty to forty families, each district had church services every two weeks. In between, a family could go to another district or invite friends to their homes to visit.

On one of these in-between Sundays, our family was invited to another family's for a Sunday dinner and a time to visit and relax. I was about fourteen at the time. They had a large family. Their oldest girl was also about the same age. I noticed that she would eyeball me at times or give me a glance now and again. I know I did the same, always trying to do so without being noticed.

It being wintertime, we stayed in the house. Us boys went upstairs and had a good time, talking about the latest events regarding school, as well as things that happened on the farm. Also, the boys were showing us oil paintings that they had gotten from a painter.

Some of the family had gone to South Dakota to a medical clinic, which was a famous place, for a lot of Amish would go for all kinds of medical ailments for treatments.

While we were looking at these truly unique paintings, a few of the oldest girls also joined us. The oldest girl sat where we could, on occasion, make eye contact. Another thing that caught her attention, that I was oblivious of, was that I wore a blue shirt with matching buttons, except one that didn't match. That morning when I put my shirt on, it was missing a button.

I remember my mother going to her button box with quite a variety of buttons. Nevertheless, she could not find a matching button. Therefore, she got a button that was the closest to the original ones. She gave the button to me and a threaded needle and asked me to sew it on. This was an ordinary task that us boys learned to do at an early age. Nevertheless, this button stood out like a sore thumb, and to this day my wife cannot forget my shirt with the mismatched button. She still gets a chuckle out of it. Well, maybe that was what it took to keep thinking of me.

Helping Each Other

Sometime in the Spring of 1936 my great-grandpa visited my folk's' home. I remember him helping my dad and older brothers shell ears of corn from our drying rack in a room upstairs for seed corn.

Learning from Each Other as a Family

It's amazing how a person can learn from each other. The Bible teaches to become as little children. Now in order to become as little children, we have to listen and observe them.

This little episode happened at the breakfast table many years ago. Yet I recall it as if it happened yesterday.

This is the arrangement in our setting at the table, which we had over many years.

Three times a day we sat at the table. Not only to eat, but it was also a time to communicate and to learn from each other— eating, praying, and communicating together.

This was our sitting arrangement: I sat at the end of the table; beside me was a high chair or a barstool, depending on the age of the child. Around the corner of the table was my wife, Orpha. This way the youngest was always between us. Therefore, it made it easier to keep the little one in control. On the left side of me and around the corner of the table was a long bench, and if it was a boy, he would graduate from the barstool to that bench and would be sitting around the corner next to me.

Now one morning Lorrie, about the age of three or four, said this as I was putting sugar on my breakfast cereal, "Dad, why do you put sugar on your cereal? It is not good for you!"

"Yes, Lorrie," I replied. "Thank you. You are right. It is not good for me, and it is not healthy. Thank you for reminding me about that. I will be happy to stop doing that."

"This will be my last bowl of cereal that I will ever eat with extra added sugar."

To this day I have not broken my promise to her and to all that were sitting around the table.

Fences

One summer my dad had a hired hand. He helped my dad fence the whole farm. The corner posts were round and I'd say about eight inches in diameter, pitch black. Us boys that tagged along were told not to touch them, or it would burn our hands.

The braces were iron from a Model T Ford undercarriage and came out of a junkyard. The posts were cemented in, and these braces were notched into the post, and the other end was cemented in a hole dug into the ground roughly twelve by eighteen by twelve inches deep.

After the brace was set in the concrete, Dad would smooth the top with a trowel. On that smooth flat surface he wrote one of our initials and the date; engraved in the concrete this particular post was this quote: ANM June 3, 1937. That was my oldest brother's initials—Amos N. Miller. The fencing had been changed over the years, yet the posts and braces looked like they did eighty years ago.

When my dad did something, he did it properly. My dad had a box wagon with four wooden wheels that a box sat in. This box was removed, and in its place was a gravel hauling box.

This box was filled with gravel. Pulling along behind was a mud boat about "three by eight feet. On it was the cement mixer and a hit-and-miss engine with a flat pulley that powered the mixer, also with a flat pulley and belt. Here was also the water barrel and a few bags of cement.

Two horses pulled this "ready mix plant" from corner to corner, installing the anchor posts.

Watering System

On the 40 acres that our friend had bought from the 154 acres, after it was fenced off. They brought all their young cattle and put them in the field.

Now, when his oldest son, Amos, and I were building the fence, Dad was developing a water system for the cattle. There was a place about one hundred feet from the new fence that water was seeping out of the ground. Dad started digging a hole about three feet deep.

He made a wooden box and set it in the hole; this box had a hole drilled close to the top of the box where he could insert a 1 ¼ inch pipe into it. This box had a two-inch plank top on it with a handle he could use to lift the top in case he wanted to check the box for some reason.

Then he dug a trench about a foot or two in depth. This trench went to the tank with the 1 ¼ pipe. The collecting box was a few feet higher than the watering tank. Therefore, as the water came up out of the ground into the collecting box and reached the pipe and ran downhill into the watering tank by the newly built fence, cattle could drink from either side of the fence.

When Amos Bontrager, who I helped build the fence, saw the water flowing through the watering tank and the overflow running into a willow patch nearby, he was struck with absolute "awe!" and amazement. He never said that he didn't believe that it wasn't going to work. Not until he saw it with his own eyes did he really believe that it would work.

He lived his young life on completely flat ground, and there were no springs. There was no water coming up out of the ground without a pump with either a windmill or a hit-and-miss engine powering the pump.

When my dad's family moved on the property, there was a flowing well on the farm on the outside of the barn. Dad later ran the water through the barn to a watering tank for the cows and horses from there to the hog house, chicken house, and wash-and-butcher house.

The house was a little higher, and it didn't run through the house. We had a pipe in the ground and a pitcher pump for the water in the house.

Syrup-Cooking

My grandpa Miller owned an eighty-acre and a fifty-acre farm that cornered at a tee road. My folks lived on the fifty acres, and my aunt's family lived on the eighty acres. On the eighty acres, there were forty acres of hardwood maple trees.

At times, us boys that did not go to school yet would hang around the sugar house, as it was called.

My dad helped gather sap water at times, or as we would call it, sugar water. It would last for about the last week in February to about the first week in April. Grandpa Miller did most of the cooking. Whenever there was a big run, they had to cook the sugar water into the night.

The most important day to us boys was the taffy-eating time. This took place each week or two. All who helped gather the sap, and at times friends and neighbors, joined together for the maple-syrup-taffy-eating.

The syrup was cooked down to a candy-type syrup and poured onto a coffee platter and eaten with a knife. A person could not eat very much at a time as it was very rich and sweet. Nevertheless, as far as a delicacy, it still would be hard to beat in my estimation.

Rabbit Tale

At about the time I started school, my oldest brother had rabbits. He let a few run loose, including a big buck. Us boys had a bad habit of teasing this buck then we would run for the henhouse, which had a screen door opening to the inside from the outside. That made for a quick getaway.

One day we were teasing him. Again, like before, when he came toward us, we hightailed it to the chicken house. Except I, being the smallest, didn't quite make it to the door. When this rabbit got ahold of my leg, he bit so hard and hung on until my older brother found a club and started hitting him. This rabbit was so determined to get even with me while he had me. To this day, if I show the children my indent in my leg, I have to confess to them that it came because us boys would torment this rabbit. It cost him his life to try to get even with me. A day or so later, this rabbit died. I knew it was my own fault, and it taught me to be more thoughtful and considerate of other living creatures.

Now, I had a very sore leg for quite a long time. I had to soak it in Epsom salt water for hours at a time, it seemed, to keep the infection out. I suffered quite a bit of pain until it finally healed. Yet the scar is still there. What hurt even more was the fact, of my foolishness, this rabbit had to die a premature death all because of our meanness and bullying. Even to this day I get a lump in my throat when I think of my stupidity of causing him to suffer and die from the injuries he got because of our tormenting him mercilessly. I know that God has forgiven us; yet there is a reaping that always comes from our acts of foolishness.

Lost Calf

On the farm in Indiana my folks milked from fifteen to eighteen cows, and in the summertime if a cow had a calf, the calves ran with the cows for about a week.

One evening the cow came home without her calf. That was extraordinarily strange. We went back to the pasture where they stayed. We found no trace of the calf. We kept our eyes open for this calf, then after we gave up hopes that this calf would ever show up.

Then one day the man that owned a forty-acre pasture field behind our land drove in our lane, and behold, he had a calf on his trailer that looked like our lost calf.

Here is the story. Several weeks earlier he came to check on his cattle. There he found this heifer with a calf alongside her. He took for granted this heifer had her calf. Therefore, he loaded them up and took them home.

This calf apparently got under the fence and ended up with the other cattle, and this heifer adopted the calf as her own. The calf primed her she became the mother. When this mother all of a sudden had two calves, he knew something was really fishy. Therefore, he brought the calf back, and the riddle was solved.

Now we know where to look, or better yet, where to put another strand of barbwire closer to the ground.

Orchard Spraying

When I was seven years old, my dad hired me out to our neighbor, Yost, which lived less than a quarter of a mile down the road from us. He had a forty-acre farm, and around ten acres of it was planted with fruit trees. He had a good-sized orchard and would sell the fruit that grew.

He also had a spraying business for the trees. He had a spray wagon with a power sprayer and a flywheel hit-and-miss engine to supply power for a three or four-hundred-gallon tank mixed with "insect powder". It had four steel wheels with a tongue and, of course, a neck yoke. Two hitched horses pulled it.

I want to mention this "insect powder". It killed the insects on contact. It had the same effect on humans, only it takes much longer to do the same thing to them.

We sat upon a wooden seat on top of the rig. Yost and I would cover about four to five-mile radius and go from place to place. Then I would drive the team between two rows of trees while he went side to side behind the sprayer. At times I'd get a good dose of overspray.

Since I had driven the team of horses for all summer, I got a lot of exposure to the spray—in particular, when the wind was blowing toward me. At times it was hard to breathe when I could not hold my breath long enough.

CHAPTER 2

※

Thankful for Health

Intravenous Infusions

I have so much to be thankful for. God has somehow spared me to this day, even though I have had to contend with this unknown poison in my body for over seventy-five years. It is the reason I am sitting in a medical-clinic room, getting intravenous transfusion treatments. The treatments help my body get rid of the poisons that I received when I was riding on top of the spray wagon, spraying poison on the fruit trees so other people could have fruit without worms.

In this session I have taken fifty three-hour treatments once a week. A few months ago, I started doing it once every two weeks. Just a word regarding these treatments: the doctors take blood tests to find the problem and then give a person a transfusion that can take as little as an hour or two. However, in my experience, it can take longer than that.

Over the years I have taken these transfusions many times. I have seen many people come and go. Also, during these times I have seen many get good results, and I have hardly ever heard anyone say that they didn't get good help. I am confident that these treatments have kept me going to this day. The clinic bridged the medical profession to the natural treatment, and I have seen many patients come in very sick and later walk out a different person.

Funeral

Yesterday we held the funeral service for our dear sister-in-law. At a still young age, she left behind her husband Loyd, their nine children and her dad and mom, Elmer and Edna Lehman-Eash. Plus numerous relatives and friends, too many to list.

Fifteen years ago, we also had a service where the last rights were held for a dear son-in-law. When everything was finished with the burial, a dear brother that lives here but could not be at the burial yesterday on account of a rare sickness that gives him a lot of almost unbearable pain, at that burial fifteen years ago this brother made the statement, loud and clear for all to hear. This is what he said, "*Do not think that Mathew is in that box! He is not in that box!*"

Yesterday sitting at the foot of the burial were three chairs, and sitting on these chairs were Marietta's father, my wife, and yours truly. Her mother could not be there also of a terminal sickness.

While they were filling the grave, I was inspired to announce, in particular for the children that were there, telling them that "Marietta is not in that box. She could very well be floating above us this very minute."

Scarlet Fever

When I was eight years old, my parents, along with many other families, contracted a dreaded disease called scarlet fever. There was a big red sign by our entry door which said *no visitors* "*quarantine*". We also were not to go anywhere there were other people.

My three-year-old sister got very sick. At the end of her scarlet fever, she also got rheumatic fever, which took her life. She was sick in bed for a very long time. From time to time Dr. Flanigan would come and check on her. It seemed to be hard on Dr. Flanigan as well as the rest of our family.

On several occasions I heard her answer when someone tried to encourage her by telling her that "someday you will get better."

She would say, "I do not want to get well." It was as if she was saying, "I am tired of being sick, and the only thing that I want is to be with Jesus." She got her wish.

Her bed not being in the living room anymore, after being there for months, was a constant reminder that she was not there anymore.

It seemed to be the hardest on our mother. It was as if she thought she didn't take proper care of her, and that might have caused her death. However, nobody ever had even an inkling of the feeling that it was our mother's fault. Many times, as she was washing dishes and her back was turned from others, I saw her wipes tears from her eyes.

On the Night She Passed from Us

Brother Melvin, the one next to her age, was awakened and brought to her side as we were all standing around her bed. She strained a little to look at him, as if to say, "Farewell. I'll see you soon." Of course, she could not speak as she was too weak and out of breath.

A little later Dad said the last words before she quit breathing. He said, "You may go to be with *Jesus. Farewell.*"

She opened her eyes wide and looked toward heaven. At that time we could not hold back any longer. We all broke down in unison. Pain and joy all mixed together. We were no longer in quarantine, and in the morning all the neighborhood boys came and did all the chores.

After the funeral, life went on; yet for me it took on a new meaning. It was corn-planting time, and when it was up several inches, my dad would cultipack the corn. Dad got me started and then went back to the dwelling. I was alone cultipacking corn. In those days, homesickness for my little sister set in. I would cry most of the time when I was alone.

A child learns to pray

The Minister

When emotions got too strong, I would stop the horses and kneel on the freshly compacted dirt and cry out to God. I did not only want to cry to him, but I did not know what to say. So I did what a minister said to me not too long before.

This is his story to the best of my memory. A farmer had a hired hand. He also had a young boy who liked to sleep longer than the older boys. When he did get up somewhat later, he always ran out behind a building and stayed there for a while.

One day the hired hand let his curiosity get the best of him. So he went out to this building and peeped around the corner. There on his knees, with his head bowed low, was this boy reciting the ABCs.

A little later the hired hand asked the young boy, "This morning I heard you behind this building, saying the ABCs. Do you care to tell me why?"

The young boy answered, "Yes, I go there every morning to pray to Jesus. I do not know what to say, so I say the ABCs for him. This way he can use those letters and say what he wants from me. I know someday he will tell me what I said."

That message from the minister about the boy inspired me to do the same. To this day I have never regretted that.

Out-of-Body Experience

I'll try to make this a short story. Nevertheless, the more I think about this, the more magnificent it seems to me.

My wife and I for the last twenty years have been taking routine physical exams. That was the way we found out that my wife had a heart condition. Whether she developed it in recent years or whether she had it from childhood, we do not know. However, during those physical exams, her heart condition was discovered; and during the course of time, it got worse. Finally, it got to the point where she had to have open-heart surgery, which took place about two and a half years ago. Today she seems to be fully recovered.

Now, since it was about five years since I had a physical, my wife urged me to take a physical, which took place in the middle of December 2011. When the results came back, the doctor read the results to me and showed me the X-rays. He informed me that nothing showed up. In fact, it was so positive he praised me for being so healthy.

Well, as it turned out, about three weeks later, while going on a stressful trip, I developed severe pain in my legs— what I took to be probably a swollen gland. I told my wife I believed if I took a hot bath, maybe the pain would go away.

After being in a tub of hot water for some time, all of a sudden I felt something unusual going on. I quickly tripped the drain lever with my toes, opened the shower slider doors, and commenced to climb out of the tub headfirst as the world was getting dark before my eyes. By keeping my head down, I obtained my sanity to a point.

It never dawned on me to call for my wife. Instead, all I could think of was, *How will I get to bed before I pass out?* I do not have much recollection of how I got to bed. All I remember was how I was floating above the mattress (in my mind).

I remember knowing that the bed and mattress was there; yet it was below me about a foot or two. I'd come and go; yet in my mind, every time I partially woke up, I was still floating always in the same position.

When I finally woke up, I found myself lying on the mattress. After lying in the same position all night long, I tried to move but couldn't at first, realizing my wife wasn't here to help me. It was our turn to open the store and since I was sound asleep. She left me sleeping while she went to the store.

After my wife came and found out what was going on, she went and got a retired registered nurse that worked at the store. She suggested that I had a blood clot in my leg. This was confirmed by the doctor later.

Hoping I didn't bore you with details when all I wanted to say was how frail our body is and how uncertain our life, no matter how healthy we are proclaimed to be.

The doctor implied that I was just one of the lucky ones that came back after having an out-of-body experience. I have a tendency to believe that my time wasn't here, of which the doctor also brought out.

All I can say to this is, Lord, if I have unfinished work to be completed or otherwise, keep me in your realm until the time is right.

The other part that I have to mention is, at some time of this ordeal, I was floating in the air above our house. I was so relaxed and in a perfect state of mind. Looking down on me lying on the bed, my knees bent a little. It was so real and no denying that it was me.

The house was completely transparent. I distinctly recall the log walls and the log ceiling joists were all very real. I was alone in bed, and I was not a bit amazed of it all. It was all very real and astounding.

The Horse Dentist

Sometime about in the midfifties, I had trouble with my wisdom teeth. Somehow I seemed to have more teeth than my mouth could handle. My local dentist advised me to pull them if they cause problems.

Therefore, he pulled them one by one, except one. He advised me to go to Fort Wayne about fifty miles from our parents' place. He said he would not be able to pull it because it was too far down or something. There he would put me to sleep, cut it out, sew it up, and charge me $50.00 for his work. I didn't like his advice and went to plan B, which was all my own idea.

This was the plan: there was another dentist in town, an older guy with his wife as his helper. He didn't have many patients as he was known to do some drinking stronger than pop. Therefore, people tended to stay away from him.

My idea was, if he couldn't do it, I could always go to this dentist in Fort Wayne later. I assumed he would explore the situation and inform me accordingly.

Instead, when I came in, he said, "How can I help you?"

I advised him that I had a wisdom tooth that was giving me problems, and I think it needed to be pulled.

He therefore informed me to get up on his chair so he could look at the problem. Now, he said this, "You are right. It needs to be pulled."

He never asked me who pulled the other three. So I didn't tell him how the others were removed.

His wife got all the necessary tools ready. He took his syringe and gave several shots around the tooth. He waited a while for that to kick in. Then he started to work on the tooth. I felt no pain and thought to myself, *Such a good dentist and all the money I will be saving.*

The next thing I heard from him were some troubling grunts and telling his wife to hand him the knife. Next I guess he started doing some cutting. All I know is they started stuffing cotton into my mouth. Then he was telling his wife how he should never have started this operation. Yet I couldn't stop now.

They—that is, the dentist and his wife—kept stuffing cotton balls in my mouth and taking out blood-saturated ones. All the while he kept cutting, prying, and pulling.

Then his pliers came out with a red chunk in its jaws. I didn't know whether it was a piece of bone or whatever. Never dawned on me that it could be a tooth until he said something like this, "I guess it came out after all!"

If he would not have said a word during the whole ordeal, I would have thought he was the best dentist in town. Instead, he had me thinking about how I was now getting to Fort Wayne to finish the job.

The only thing that I could do now was to give him his agreed fee of $4.00 and shaking his hand in approval and gratification for his good work. My mouth was stuffed with cotton balls. Therefore, no words were spoken.

CHAPTER 3

The People We Meet

People of All Walks of Life

Over the years we have attracted many people in all walks of life. We have met good and bad people, from poor to rich ones, from beggars to extortionists, and everything in between.

I'll attempt to describe one that came to Rexford, Montana, in our early years. It was a young family with two children. They drove in with an old pickup truck that was loaded down like *The Beverly Hillbillies* truck that carried their belongings to Hollywood.

We all thought, "Just who were these people that came to our community, and what were they looking for?"

The answer is as complicated as the question. They all came for a reason and a purpose that was as wide and long as your imagination. Some came to work and hunt and fish. There was a variety of different reasons, such as finding a better environment for their boys to grow up in.

The one question everyone had on their mind was, "What do these people want from us that would benefit them?"

I'll give you another example. A lonesome man stopped in at our place and claimed to be in the blackcap raspberry business. He wanted to know if there was a place here that he could stay for the night with hopes of having a meeting to discuss the business. We did let him stay.

We had an empty cabin close to our house where he stayed for the night. He also had a Doberman Pinscher that was such a vicious dog nobody ventured to get close to him.

That evening we held a meeting for him at the schoolhouse so he could present his blackcap Raspberry business. At least he meant no harm, but his beat-up truck, his vicious dog, and his less-than-dressed-up appearance left us with some unanswered questions.

He bought some dog food at our store and then settled down in our cabin until it was time for the meeting at the schoolhouse. If I remember correctly, he wanted to sell blackcap raspberry plants for us to raise. Then he would buy the raspberries back and marketed the same.

After the meeting, he again settled down in the cabin. Now this was our mistake; it never dawned on us that the man had nothing to eat but dog food. For this oversight, we still regret this to this day, even though we have repented for this simple oversight. We have always been more conscious of other people's situations that they face ever since.

Nonetheless, this man ate dog food and got very sick. He apparently thought this dog food was poisonous; therefore, he ate charcoal from the stove. He didn't cool it enough and burned his mouth and throat. We heard a commotion from the basement, so we went down to see what was going on. We found the man with a water hose in his mouth, trying to cool his burning lips, mouth, and throat.

We sent word to some of the neighbors about the situation, and we decided to call the sheriff to help us figure out what to do. The hospital was ninety miles away in Kalispell, Montana, and the man needed immediate help. Plus, to add to the situation, there was his dog to contend with. The dog was sitting in a pouncing position, snarling and showing his teeth to let everyone know he meant business if any of us got too close.

The man seemed to get sicker by the minute. He still had the water hose in his mouth and was soaked from limb to limb. Also, the man had a bad case of diarrhea. He was standing above the floor drain, dripping wet and diarrhea running out of his pant legs.

Imagine the sheriff and his deputy walking into such a sight. I heard the sheriff say to his deputy, with a grin on his face, "These people seem to have a magnet to draw in these types of people to them." The deputy agreed by giving an understanding grin back to him. The law officers were very understanding and told us that they would take the man and his dog back to town and then determine what to do.

We thanked them and apologized for the trouble we caused them. We even offered to pay for a hotel room and any other expenses that might incur. They indicated that would not be necessary. The officers were very gracious and assured us that they were only trying to help and this was their job.

Changing Beliefs as We Learn

Building log homes as a means of what is called "making a living"—this at times took us around different parts of the country. I was the one that made the sales. This was to be our last sale before turning the business over to the boys.

We were—that is, my wife and I—traveling by train and came to Sacramento, California, where for some reason we had to change trains. We had several hours layover, so we took the city transit bus and visited restored old Sacramento and came back in plenty of time to board the train for Portland, Oregon. Boarding time was 9:00 p.m. When boarding time arrived, there was an announcement made, informing the passengers they had engine problems. However, it was expected that it would take about an hour to fix the problem.

When the hour was up, another announcement was made, stating that they did not get the problem remedied yet. It could take an additional hour to make the repairs. Apologizing for the delay, this kept going on hour after hour. This was a real test of the people's patience. Some chewed out the personnel behind the glass. One lady came up to the glass, and while she was chewing out, the people behind the glass, one of the clerks, reached up and pulled the Venetian blinds. Now she was staring at the blinds between them.

As is accustomed with those glasses that separate the passengers from the train personnel, the glass had a slot about a foot wide and maybe inches tall. This lady reached in through this slot and got ahold of the blinds and pulled the blinds right out through the slot. This only explains the setting: lots of commotion going; not much thought of who really is in charge of the circumstances, or you might say, who is responsible to give us the opportunity for us to be here in the first place, let alone the thought that unless we recognize our maker and our savior, Jesus Christ, our opportunities are short-lived.

I wrote all this to come to what this subject is all about. The seating was arranged so that there were two sets of seating facing each other, with an isle maybe about eight to ten feet between the seating. My wife and I were sitting in the front row. Right across from us were two gentlemen. They were talking nonstop all the while we were waiting for the train to be ready to leave.

We could hear just enough to know they were talking about the Bible. It seemed that each was trying to get their point across, but nobody was winning the argument. Nobody was mad, yet they both seemed extremely serious about the points that they were making. They talked nonstop all night long.

By early morning, they got the engine going, and we boarded the train headed for Portland, arriving there in the evening, of course missing our connection in Portland. Therefore, they put us up in a motel for the night to catch the next train for our destination. The next morning we went for breakfast in a big dining room as part of the motel. As we walked in the dining room, we walked by a table that had two gentlemen sitting, the same people that sat across the aisle from us at the train station. They were still talking nonstop. We greeted them with a "Good morning." They looked at us and returned the greeting.

We had a leisurely breakfast and were leaving the dining room and again came to this table where the two gentlemen were still talking nonstop. I made a comment, and they asked if we wouldn't mind joining them.

I looked at my wife, and she said, "You can join them while I write a letter."

The conversation went something like this. The first gentleman explained himself something like this. I have been raised and became a leader in a major religious denomination. Although, he didn't say so in that many words, but nevertheless, I could detect that he was a strongly religious person.

Now, the other gentleman introduced himself. All he said was that he also belonged to a different religious denomination.

Now it was my turn. I do not recall the exact words that I used, only to say that I grew up with a different religious background, and I believe in my Lord and Savior, Jesus Christ. I did ask the second gentleman for a testimony regarding his faith.

He went into quite detail in how he was raised and taught the importance of his church. He lived and believed it. Later in life he took life seriously and went to work for the cause of the church. He dug deep to find all the ground that he could to defend his cause. However, the more he dug to defend his cause, the more he discovered that he was working for the wrong cause.

After many trials and tribulations, he came to realize he had to completely change his thinking, taking his complete life to the cross of Jesus. There at the cross, he found a renewing of his mind and began a new course. Losing all that was so dear to him. What a sobering defeat. He had to suffer. Most all that he had been taught and was teaching was all in vain and had all to come to nothingness. Not only did he lose his former beliefs, he lost most of his friends and his reputation in the church. He became ridiculed and shunned. He also became a priest, yet a priest of a different nature; a priest of all believers. The life he now lives is not his life.

He said 'he had nothing to boast about himself; he lost all that he had but the cross. He could only boast about Jesus living in him.

Then he turned to me and said, "I have given my testament to the best of my knowledge. Now I wouldn't mind hearing your testament."

Now it was my turn to expose myself. On one end, he inspired me to testify. On another note, he took the wind out of my sails. Since we grew up on very similar teachings, I could easily comprehend his understanding and how sure he was that in his opinion, his church was the only church that had the chance to get to heaven. Whereas I was just as confident that I had the right teaching and that my church was the one that was on the right track, and all others just didn't get it.

I, too, had to have my motives changed through many trials and tribulations. Only after surrendering myself at the foot of the cross, losing it all for the sake of Christ, becoming a nobody, losing all my dignity and being rejected by the ones closest to me, trampled underfoot, ridiculed, and shunned, if Christ wouldn't have come to my rescue I could have despaired.

Now it didn't matter anymore. I was as low as a person can go, and whatever more was coming my way didn't make one bit of difference since I was as low as I could go. Besides, since I was now dead to myself, there was nothing anybody could do. It doesn't benefit anybody to kick a dead man. Also, it was no longer me but Christ living in me. Therefore, I reasoned if they were going to keep on kicking, the one they were kicking had been kicked before, and he could handle it.

While I was trying to explain or give my testament, telling it was very similar to his. I noticed that this other person was shaking and silently sobbing, and tears were running down his cheeks. All of a sudden he couldn't hold it any longer. Raising his hands in the air, he exclaimed very emphatically, "Lord, help *me, a sinner!*" Now his outstretched hands came down on the table, along with his face flat on the table.

He said, "*Please pray for me!*" Now he was sobbing out loud and didn't seem to care who heard him while we prayed for him.

He had been thoroughly convicted where he stood and what he believed. Having been blinded to the truth and realizing it was more than he could handle. When he realized his unbelief and cried out to God, he was touched by the spirit, and he couldn't help himself.

I have never met the man since. Yet I have no doubt that he found joy. I have no doubt should I chance to run across his path, I would find out that he changed his priesthood order from an earthly priest to a spiritual priest, joining the priesthood of all believers.

Visiting a Japanese Family in Seattle

One of the Japanese businessmen that we met had a family that included him, his wife, and three girls. They lived in Seattle and invited us over for a visit and provided room and board for us.

We accepted the invitation. We ate the evening meal and breakfast with them. We had a very nice visit with them. Talking about their lodge, it seemed to be working out great for them. They have invited us to stay at the lodge, but so far, it has never happened.

Blackout

They also talked about a three-day blackout that occurred in the city of Seattle. I believe it happened around the late 'eighties or 'nineties.

Talk about chaos. Imagine no electricity, no water, no gas! Unless you had a tank full of gas in your car, you only went as far as you could walk. Even if you had enough gas to get out of town, all the gas stations were either out of gas or were packed with a long line of cars trying to get in. *Nuff said!*

Back to the Seattle Visit

Now, going back to the Japanese family we were visiting. They told us about life in their house in America. The girls were in school for the most part of their life. When they came home from school, they mostly went up to their rooms. They would come down long enough to eat their meal that their mother prepared with great care. After eating, they would go back upstairs.

In the morning they came down long enough to grab a bite to eat and headed off to school. This was their life until the blackout happened. That changed everything; no more upstairs life, except to sleep.

For the first time they all sat in the living room and visited as a family. The girls learned how to cope without the electric gadgets and all ease that comes with that. They also realized, in part, what is lost by living upstairs by themselves and their gadgets.

The parents realized how precious it is to have a family sitting together in the living room, learning from each other instead of listening to other people speak or the wild music that comes with it. Maybe a "blackout" day or two would be good for all of us.

The Dentist

To give a little history of why I had to go to this dentist or how I came into contact with him, he said he comes to our store frequently. Yet I had never really met him one-on-one.

This episode started in fall 1975. I was removing a wheel from a piece of equipment. It had ¾-inch bolts with rusted threads from years of use. You guessed the rest. Even though I had soaked them with WD40 and had a long-handled wrench, I worked hard to get the nuts off. One time, when I was pulling up with all of my strength, the wrench came up and hit my jaw. It didn't completely knock me out. The first thing that I could remember was that I was spitting out pieces of teeth.

Over the years I have had to fix these teeth. Finally, I had enough, and they became unfixable. So I had them pulled. In the process the dentist broke my jawbone in order to get the root out. When that was finally healed, I was advised to see this dentist that I am writing this episode about.

This dentist is some seventy years young. As well as being a good dentist, he also is a man full of knowledge, with a lot of on-hand experience. This man has a lot of positive things to say with well-balanced-out negative realities. One thing led to another, and the conversation came to discipline, much caused by split-up families. He had worked in a prison for some six or eight years, once a week, in the women's ward. He said that close to 100 percent of the women in that ward were the fruits of broken families.

Now, this is what I want to write about. My wife and I were traveling on the train some twenty years ago. They put us in the handicap car downstairs. There were around twenty or thirty people in the car, mostly older and one young mother with an unruly and spoiled two to three-year-old brat, yelling and screaming for the least little thing that didn't go his way.

On the train was a man, eighty-four years old, very good-natured but full of spunk. Finally, he had enough. He got up and walked to her seat and exclaimed, very forcefully and emphatically, "Lady, if you do not put some discipline in that child, that child will end up in jail!"

She left the car and never came back.

To that the dentist commented, "Today that child is probably in jail."

This is why that lady had no clue about discipline. She had no idea what he was talking about. Therefore, she could do nothing to correct the situation. Now he explained what happened in her life, raised in a nonfunctional home and in a nonfunctional community with no one to teach her the principles of life.

In a family, there has to be at least one grandmother to look to for guidance. If that link in the chain that holds the family and community is broken or missing, it leaves the doors wide open for Satan to come in and tear the family apart.

Turtle Dove

Later in life there were times when we had all kinds of people come into our meetings. Most had a good sermon. Yet there were things that caused much concern. In the course of time, this caused much unrest and turmoil. It was heartbreaking to see all this taking place with seemingly nothing to do about it. All the pleading and praying seemed to fall on deaf ears.

One day, as I was working in the mill yard, sorting logs with the skid-steer loader, I was meditating about all that was going on and having no solution to the problem. I remember I was just sitting on the loader, thinking about the whole situation, feeling letdown and left out with no one to go to and no one to discuss the matter with. Just then a turtle dove landed on the frame of the forks, which are connected to the forks on the loader. This frame comes up within a foot or so of my knees. I could almost reach out and touch the dove sitting on the frame. I thought, surely, if I move, it would fly off. Nevertheless, it just sat there. Surely, if I move the loader, it will fly away. I started moving slowly to not scare it too bad, but it just kept sitting there. I gathered up a load of logs and dumped them on the sawmill deck, and this bird just hung on. Several times if I jerked too hard or moved too fast, it fought hard to hang on. Then after several loads this bird ever so gracefully flew up and sat on top of the sawmill building. Later it flew away.

All I can say is, no matter how bad things seem to be, he is always at hand. Sometimes we make it hard for him to hold on. Yet he is persistent and never lets go or gives up.

Borrowing watermelons

Town Marshal

In the year 1954 I was drafted to go to the service. Sometime in the thirties or early forties, a law was passed stating that a believer that on account of his religious beliefs as a pacifist, he could register as a conscientious objector.

In the years leading up to that year as a teenager, a lot of tall tales were floating around. Here is one that stuck with me. The town of Topeka had a man put in charge to keep order in town. They called him the marshal. Since there wasn't much to do in that department, he had a lot of time on his hands in which case he made up with the Amish boys. Whenever he could, of course. The boys also found him "interesting," to put it lightly. They liked to play tricks on him since he was lacking. Should I say, as the saying goes, he was "missing a few marbles."

Since he was in charge of "watching out for thieves etc.", they thought they would put him to the test.

One evening, as they were fun-lovingly having a good time, one of the boys suggested, "Why don't we get us a few watermelons and have a feast?"

"Yah," everyone chimed in. "That's a good idea! Let's go to the Harry Bontrager cornfield right by the road. There are a lot of watermelons in that cornfield. He surely wouldn't miss just a few melons."

This was what took place. One of the boys had sneaked his dad's shotgun along. Going off a little way from the other boys and the marshal, there he shot in the air and started to cry, "Help! Help!"

This marshal took off for his car like a scared rabbit right back to town as fast as he could go, thinking that the farmer caught them and hit one of them with a shotgun.

Now, after they quit laughing, they realized they were on foot and they had better start walking. When the marshal found out it was all a "scam," he had the last laugh! Because they all had to walk home.

My Last Dress

About the year 1914, traveling from Phoenix, Arizona, by way of California, we stopped in Bonners Ferry, Idaho, for a short rest and to eat at a restaurant there.

As we had settled in eating our dinner, a man and his wife walked by our table. They gave up an understanding greeting. We returned the same and could easily see that they were Anabaptists.

When we finished eating, we walked over to their table and introduced ourselves. We learned that they were also from Indiana and LaGrange. Also, his first name was the same as mine and that as a boy, we ate—that is, my parents and family—were invited to their house for a meal.

It also dawned on me that his mother gave a dress to my mother to me for my namesake. I confess that I do not remember wearing that dress. However, I do remember the color of it and that it was a long dress for a two or three-year-old. In those days, boys wore dresses up to three years old or older.

Some people might think that to be weird for a boy to wear a dress. Nevertheless, we had a picture of the president, John Kennedy, and his wife and family. A little boy holding hands with his mother, Jackie; the little boy, John John, which he was called, was wearing a dress.

My take is this: if a president's boy can wear a dress, down-to-earth country farm boys should feel good in following a president's boy's footsteps.

Halloween Stunts

I also might mention on the night of Halloween there was always some interesting happenings taking place. One time a farmer found his young bull in the haymow.

Word got around, and the whole neighborhood came over to see what was going on. As they stood around, scratching their heads, trying to figure out how he got up there and how to get him down, it seemed like no one could come up with a solution.

Then all of a sudden one of the grown boys thought of something like this. What might be the chances of running one of the barn doors off the tracks and setting it on a slant against the haymow and sliding him down it? That sounded like a plan.

That also solved the mystery of how he got up there by the marks already there when they dragged him up there. What a great discovery by the boy who thought of how to get him down!

Moving the Outhouse 'Four Feet Back!

Take this one with a grain of salt.

Supposedly a man had his outhouse tipped over every year. Therefore, he figured out a way to stop it. So, on the day of Halloween, he moved the house back about 'four feet. Needless to say, that was the last time that he found his house tipped over. Also, it was still standing in the morning after he pushed it back.

Now I never heard how the pushers made out of their surprise. I can only imagine they had a surprise of their life, and the owner found the evidence by the footprints in the heaps of the product of the remains!

CHAPTER 4

Seventy-Acre Farm

Carp Recipe

From 1962 to 1972 we lived on a seventy-acre farm. A creek ran into a small lake on the back side of the property. In the spring the river would always overflow and flood the marsh that surrounded the lake. The creek connected two lakes about a mile apart from each other. In the spring of the year this creek would overflow into the marshland. At times the water was six to ten inches deep in the marshland.

Carp could be caught in these waters. The fish, Carp, was hardly edible. Rumor was that there was only one way to use or prepare the fish. Here is the method: they had to be gutted, skinned, and put on a cedar board. Then you leave the fish on the board for three days in the sun. At the end of that time, you throw the fish to the hogs or chickens.

If perhaps you would like to find out how the fish tastes, all you have to do is lick the board clean. If you should venture to try it, I am convinced you will have accomplished two things; this will be your first and last Carp episode all in one venture.

Sweet Corn

On account of the creek, marshland, and lakes, there was only about twenty-eight acres of farmland. Twenty-eight acres was not enough land to have a normal farming operation. Therefore, we were looking for ways to supplement the farm with other means.

We always had a big garden, a few milk cows, and a few hogs. One day I went to the only neighbors that lived close to us. I enjoyed visiting with the older gentleman and his son that lived there. They were old-time farmers. They farmed and planted strictly by the almanac. The conversation went something like this:

"Well," he said, "it sure is a nice day. What did you do today?"

"Well," I said, "I did this and that, and we also planted our sweet corn."

"Oh!" he said. "This is not the time to plant corn! It will not produce any corn. The almanac says the sign is in the root. Therefore, you will not get any corn."

I thought about telling him that we did not plant the corn in the "sign"; we planted it in the ground. However, I didn't tell him that.

This is what happened: we had more corn than we could eat, so we put a shingle out with *Sweet Corn* on it. We sold it quickly and could have sold much more. So, by accident, this put a thought in our mind, and we started our sweet-corn business. To some extent, this business has lasted to this day.

Whoops, missed the pile

Planer Shavings

Also, in the third year in the fall, we built a broiler house to supplement the farm. A few years later we bought shavings from a planer mill for bedding for the chickens. The truck driver dumped the load of shavings in front of the building by the door. The second floor of the building had a door above the bottom door.

We had three children at this time. We were very busy and were not keeping close attention on what they were up to. The two oldest, Arlene and Ervin, were jumping from the second floor into the pile of shavings.

Since they were having so much fun, the youngest, Loyd, also wanted to have fun like his older sister and brother. However, being only two or three years old, he couldn't jump out far enough and pretty much landed on the ground. That was when we heard the commotion. We quickly ran to see what was going on and what we needed to do.

There was no need to lock the door after the horses were stolen. Nevertheless, it taught us to be more cautious of what the children were up to!

Agriculture to Sawmill

A little history, which I take no pleasure in writing about; yet if a person wants to refer back to history, the disappointing things have to be written as well as the more exciting things.

Looking back, we did not discover the property that we moved to. My background was agriculture in nature. Nevertheless, having a small farm, time was filled in with construction work. Therefore, I had some knowledge in the building trade. This place in Montana was far removed from any construction work, and farming was not an option. Therefore, as timber was all around us, something in the line of lumber seemed to be the best option.

We looked around to buy a sawmill and found one where the owner wanted to quit. He worked more for the mill than it was worth. Yet he had a big contract with a railroad tie-treating plant. With that contract, it made the deal seem valid.

We made the deal and commenced to disassemble the mill and reassemble it again. We built a building, and in a couple months, we were sawing logs into railroad ties.

Not ever having sawed any logs before, it took a lot of elbow grease and a lot of patience until it was running smoothly. We finally got most of the kinks and quirks worked out, and all seemed to come together, and all seemed to run smoothly.

But alas! How things can change without notice. One Sunday morning the boys were outside when they saw smoke coming from the sawmill. We all ran back to the mill. It was far too late to do any good. The whole building was pretty much on fire. The walls were falling in, and the roof was collapsing. The acetylene tanks were pushed over, and the heads were broken off. The gas was spewing out in full force on the big diesel engine, melting it beyond anything but junk. As devastating as it seemed and how hard it was to believe that after all that work—and not only that, but everything that we had accumulated up to that time went up in smoke—all we could do was to put it in God's hands and let him handle it. We knew how he had come through in times past, and we knew he would do it again. This time there were no lives lost, only material mater. All that could be replaced in time. Lord willing!

Nevertheless, this caused extreme hardships. Being in a place where nothing was close, it was sixty miles to the closest machine shop. A lot of things like that caused costs to overrun.

We were investing heavily in timber sales, and now no means to harvest the timber. Nevertheless, God was merciful. The Forest Service, where the timber contract was made, extended our time to harvest it. A good neighbor helped in setting up a new mill. What had appeared to be an impossible task turned out to be a rich blessing. We can only give God the credit and any glory for bringing this about.

In saying *we*, that includes my wife and I, our sons and daughters, plus a host of good neighbors, plus an understanding banker.

Giving back to God, a Dear Son and Brother

In around the year 1955, the county of LaGrange in the town of LaGrange, they built a new hospital; and thereafter, the doctors no longer came to the homes to deliver babies. If you wanted them to be a part of the delivery, you had to bring them to the hospital. Therefore, all our children were born in the hospital.

The fifth child was one of them. They had a small room for the husbands to stay while the delivery was taking place. For me, that was always a dreaded place to be—away from the action and not knowing what was going on.

This time it was no different. When they finally let me go in, I right away detected that all was not well.

Orpha's eyes were filling with tears when she saw me. The loud gurgling and rattling in the baby's throat were more than I could handle, no matter how hard I tried to be strong for her. For a long time not a word was spoken. Then the nurse broke the silence. She said this, "The doctor will be in shortly to advise you on what they are planning to do."

This is what the doctor told us, "I have called a specialist in Fort Wayne and made an appointment for you to take him there because it is beyond our means to help him in this hospital. Hopefully, by tomorrow you will be strong enough to go."

We arranged for a driver to pick us up in the morning. It was fifty miles and took about an hour. A nurse came and took him away. He was gone for what seemed the longest time.

The nurse handed the baby to Orpha. He was still making the same noise or sound. Also, the same struggle to get air.

Now the doctor spoke, and this is what he said. He was very kind and tried his best to bring the news as gently as he could. Nevertheless, he explained what caused his struggle to get enough air intake to keep him going.

He explained that his trachea was not properly developed. Instead of being like a radiator hose, it was more like (his term) a gunny sack, in a language that we understood.

"He would have to have surgery to remedy the problem. However, it would be too much for him. He could not survive the operation. Therefore, I'm sorry to have to inform to you, which you probably have concluded. To us it is very obvious that to all of our regrets, it is the truth of the matter. The best you can do is to recognize the obvious. Take him home and love and enjoy him as long as you can. Then give him back to God where he no longer has to suffer."

The doctor knew the mother watching him suffer in trying to get air was even harder than just letting him go. So this kept on going for twenty-four hours a day for a month, never knowing when he might take his last breath.

That last breath didn't come until almost nine years later—at a time least expected—not from lack of oxygen from a dysfunctional windpipe but from a fall from a spring wagon onto the blacktop road. This was caused by a runaway horse going around a corner at full tilt, pitching our son and brother headfirst onto the hard surface, instantly taking his life.

Many people that read this will understand when I say words cannot describe the pain that is caused by having a dear tenderhearted young son or daughter instantly taken away.

However, there is an exception to every rule. In our family there was one dear one that could not force one tear during the funeral.

As much as I would like to weep with the rest of the family and others as well, as hard as I tried, I could not force one teardrop. I did not know what was wrong.

I believe what had happened with Vernon was, it was the same with his life. Do you remember? Or do you not?

Vernon never cried. The first part of his life he couldn't cry. At times, I know that he wanted to, but nevertheless, it was hard enough to try to breath without crying. He could not breath and cry at the same time. Therefore, he gave up trying to cry. That matter kept with him the rest of his life.

So it is with you. You suffered with him for hours, days, nights, weeks, and months, yes and even years. That made such an impact on your life.

Now that all that is over, inwardly you are rejoicing. That that has become into fulfillment, and it brings so much inner enjoyment it chokes out any desire to weep.

God gave you that ability; therefore, let us rejoice and thank him for it.

CHAPTER 5

Everyday Happenings

Forward on Happenings

As we go through life of everyday living, we come across some unusual happenings. Some are thought-provoking, some have brought many tears, some of joy, and some of sorrow. Other times it brought trials and tribulations in sickness and health. The list could go on and on. Yet, in all these things, if our eyes are fixed on Jesus, it only helps us to make our calling more secure.

The Refrigerator

One spring evening in the first half of the 'sixties, we were at the threshold of a major tragedy.

This was it. The house and barn were close together. In front of the house was an enclosed porch with screen doors at each end. It served as an entry to the house. On this entryway was an ice box, which served as a refrigerator in the summertime. It had two doors, one on top big enough to hold one hundred pounds of ice and a big door below it for food.

We had three children: Arlene, Ervin, and Lloyd—with Lloyd being about three years old. Children can think of a lot of things to do, including taking all the racks out of the refrigerator and crawling inside.

Yes, you guessed it, Lloyd shut the door! Yet he could not open it when he heard the screaming inside. He panicked and managed to climb on top of the refrigerator by means of shelving on the wall at the end of the refrigerator.

That in itself didn't open the door; yet his loud screams carried farther being on top of the refrigerator.

Mom, hearing his screams, came to the rescue and opened the door where two, wet, soaked-from-sweating children tumbled out on the floor, almost breathless yet soon revived; yet very, very scared in not knowing if Mom would hear his cry in the barn where she was milking.

Those older-model refrigerators could not be opened from the inside. Today, if I see a refrigerator with an outside latch, I take the latches off right away.

An example: our boys bought an old-fashioned commercial refrigerator that had about six doors with outside latches. They used it for a storage unit in their shop. I took all the latches off and threw them away.

Worshiping with the Cattle

ORA MILLER

Worshiping with the Cattle

On occasion we have our Sunday service in a pavilion close to the community building where we normally gather.

This time an "I'll call him a preacher," from a distance came. He had the opening in the service. This was the setting.

Across the road was a field that kept a herd of cattle. These cattle were crowding the fence and mooing a nonharmonic choir. This preacher took special attention to their mooing with their heads all toward our open building. He was so moved he couldn't resist in commenting in the interest they showed in our gathering. Something like this is what he said.

"Today I've seen it all. I knew this was an anointed place. However, this is the first I've ever seen the cattle assemble along with us and join in with the worship service."

"I knew that the Holy Spirit was in the people, yet this is the first time that it got into the cattle as well."

Now, I'll tell you the "rest of the story." What this preacher didn't know was that we—that is, my wife and I—have a golf cart that we use to get around in the community, and that was what we used to come to the meeting.

We also use this cart to feed our cattle the trimmings and pumice that we get from making apple butter and apple cider.

Therefore, whenever we drive around the community close to the field where the cattle are, they come running toward us, figuring we will feed them their dessert.

That is what happened the morning of the service. We went by the field, turned the corner, and drove to where the service was held. The cattle saw the cart. Now, if the cattle could think, they probably thought if they beg enough, they might bring us some juicy apple trimmings and pumice.

Now, instead of apples, they got a sermon. End of story.

Homemade Softball

The local feed mill was just down the road about a mile. Sometimes us boys would go along with Dad to the mill. They had a barrel that they threw the strings in that had been used to sow the feed sacks shut.

To us boys this was a treasure barrel with all the strings that we needed to make softballs. Whenever a cover came off of a softball in school, or one of our homemade softballs got knocked around to where it needed a new interior, we used this string to make a new interior and sowed the cover back on.

These homemade balls didn't fly as far as the store-bought ones, yet they served our purpose and saved Dad's money.

Slop Bucket

This episode took place in the sixties. My wife, Orpha, had to run some errands. She stopped at the home of the Lester and Clara Hostetler farm. In those days, every farm home had what was called a slop bucket or slop pail (schlop ehma).

Orpha tied her horse to the hitching rail and walked toward the house. It was dark, and they had a door that opened to an enclosed porch. Since this door was a ways from the inside door that opens to the house, she thought she had better go inside and knock on the interior door.

The door opened, and a head popped out, exclaiming, "Did you empty the slop pail?" ("Hust du da schlop ehma aus geluid?")

Clara had heard the door open and thought it was Lester.

This incident caused many a chuckle, including in the year 2007 when we had our fiftieth wedding anniversary. I was playing shuffleboard with some other man. There was a fence behind us. When I heard a voice call my name, I looked around, and there standing on the other side of the fence were two women, their hands on the fence and looking toward me.

One of them said, "Do you know me?"

I had to think for just a moment, and then it came to me. I addressed her by her name that was given when someone wanted to make sure they had the right Clara in mind.

I exclaimed, "Yes, you are Sam, John's, Ervins, Clara!"

To which I also should have told her that Orpha still hasn't emptied the slop bucket.

The Thorn in Our Side

In the twelfth chapter of 2 Corinthians focusing on verse 7 he talks about a thorn in the flesh put there by Satan to buffet him lest he should be exalted above measure on account of the many revelations that were given him. My understanding is, God used Satan as an instrument to keep Paul from being exalted—opposite of Satan's purpose.

I will use my older brother to give somewhat of an example of what Paul made so clear. That is, God will do things or have things happen in ways to keep us humble and not to be exalted.

My brother had gifts and revelations in many areas and, on account of these gifts and revelations, caused him a lot of what we would call "headaches". By the time he was in first grade, the bullies and leaders of the flock were jealous of him.

Therefore, they gave him nicknames and slandered him in all kinds of ways, telling him he would never amount "to a hill of beans" and much more. I could write a book of the many things that he did in his lifetime. Yet I will only mention one happening.

Now I want to mention that he is not with us anymore. Going home from a meeting, he accidently drove in front of a truck, and it took his life. He went home to glory instead.

Broken Record

One Sunday in his midteens, my older brother and a few others went to a friend's house where the boy lived with the rest of the family. His friend had a record player, an old hand-cranked record player called a Victrola.

Somehow in the process of playing the records, one of them slipped out of his hand and on the floor, and it broke. Therefore, my brother told him he would get him another one to replace it. So that was what he did. Soon thereafter he went to town and bought another record to replace the one that he broke. Now he had this new record in his possession, which was a 78-rpm record but without a way to play it before he gave it to his friend for the one he broke.

Most anybody with such a situation would quickly and not even think of a way to play a record without a proper machine. Well, like I said, that was not him. He would think of something like this.

He was thinking of how he might figure out a way to play this record. If only someone made a record and thought of a way to make it play with a needle hooked up to an object that could pick up sound.

Therefore, first he had to make a contraption that would turn the record, which was about ten inches in diameter and about one eighth of an inch thick with a hole in the center about one half of an inch.

Then he thought of the separator, which was in the milk house. That was what he did. These were called cream separators. At that time most older farmers had one of them and would know how it works. It had a stem projecting from out of the gear case where the bowl was connected. It had a hand crank and a spindle that was turned by the crank. When the crank was turned, the stem turned, which turned the separating bowl. This spindle had a slot at the top about one half inch deep about the width of a nickel. Now, on top of this spindle, he made a plate with heavy cardboard with a deal fabricated to fit into this slot and also a pinup through the cardboard the size of the hole in the record. Now, if you laid the record on top of this cardboard and turned the crank of the separator, this record turned and could be speed adjusted by the speed of the crank.

Now he had to figure out how to get the sound out of the record and bring the sound to life. In other words, an audible sound. Since he didn't have a loud speaker to attach it to, he got one of mother's needles and stuck this needle through the eraser of a new lead pencil at about a thirty-degree slant. The sound got picked up by the needle as the needle glided in the groove of the record as someone turned the crank of the separator, and the sound went through the pencil that was held by the teeth of the listener. This sound was as clear as a record player to the one that held the pencil between his or her teeth.

Turning the crank was my job in playing our first record. I can still recall the smile on his face as he finished his first record-playing experiment.

Now it was his turn to turn the crank and let me see if he was just trying to play a joke on me or if that smile was for real. Well, how it amazed me is saying it lightly. I had no idea how clear the sound was. Not only was it clear, it engulfed my whole body and soul.

Not only did I smile when I had my turn, I felt like screaming out loud. How such a simple apparatus could make such a clear sound go through your body yet hardly making a sound to a person standing close by is hard to explain?

Therefore, this became a homemade record player created from a hand-crank cream separator. Needless to say, this new-found invention never needed a patent. Only us boys and a few of our friends got a kick out of our brother's invention.

The Ditch

As I mentioned in Chapter 1, my grandad's ditch was dug to go around the mint farm, but this ditch had other uses besides draining the land, however, in a much-lesser degree.

In the summertime the uncles and aunts would gather at Grandpa's farm several times a year. It was agreed among us boys that whoever came there first would place planks in front of the culvert to stop the water from flowing through it. This caused the water to rise and became our summer swimming hole.

Cousins

The next episode that I clearly remember was when my older brother and I took our Red Ryder Wagon to our cousin's house one evening. They lived less than a quarter mile down the road from us, so we played together often.

We had no particular mission in mind. We were just wanting to play. As we got to the front door, we saw them in the living room, sitting and playing. They did not notice us there, so my brother and I decided to play a trick on them. This is what happened...

We knocked on the door and quickly hid behind the bushes. They came to the door and found no one there. We waited a while and then went to the door and opened it to go inside. To our surprise, they all let out a loud scream. We got so scared we quickly retreated and ran for home.

When they realized it was just us, they hollered after us to come back. Needless to say, we were quite a ways down the road by then, but we heard them and had to walk all the way back just to play. Well, that trick backfired on us.

That was the last time we had any desire to play that kind of a trick on my cousins or anyone else. They were home alone, and we scared the wits out of them. The looks on their faces and their horrified screams still haunts us to this day.

First Soda

Yost and I were headed toward a small country store. He told me we'd stop there and get us a soda. I didn't have a clue what a soda was! I mulled it over in my mind and decided it might be a cake because I remembered that sometimes Mother would add soda to her bake dough.

I had been in this store a number of times, yet I had never sat on one of those swivel stools. If I had been alone, I would have taken a few rides on this neat swivel stool.

Now, we sat there and the owner, Howard, came over and asked, "What can I do for you?"

Yost answered, "I'll take a Coke."

Now, Yost threw a monkey wrench in my train of thought. He changed his order from a soda to a Coke. Now I don't know what Coke was nor did I know what a soda was.

I finally said, "I'll have the same."

Howard turned around and opened a door on the wall that was stacked with all kinds of glassware. He pulled out two funny-looking glasses. These glasses had about a three-inch-diameter flat stand and a glass stem about 3/8-inch thick and about four inches to the bottom of an oval-shaped bottom for a total of six to seven inches tall. Howard held these glasses by the stem under a sort of nozzle and a small pipe with a handle. He pulled the handle down, and out came a dark liquid. The portion of about two tablespoons full. Next he held one at a time under another nozzle. He filled these stem glasses by pulling another lever down, and out gushed a small stream of liquid, causing a foam in the glass. This liquid made a hissing sound as the glass filled.

The next thing Howard did was put a stick in it to stir it. I noticed it was hollow, and that stumped me. I quickly peeked over to see what Yost was doing with his hollow stick. I saw that he had it in his mouth, and it appeared as if he might be sucking on it, instead of blowing into it to mix it up like I was going to do.

Therefore, I thought I'd try that and see what happens. What happened was the surprise of my life, to put it mildly. For some reason, I imagined it would come out hard, so I gave a good hard suck and inhaled.

The next thing I knew, something awful and burning was coming out of my nose, and some went into my lungs. I sure was lucky that the store was not full of people; otherwise, somebody would have come to my rescue. They would have quickly had me on the floor to give me emergency resuscitation.

After I recovered from the main attack, Howard kindly said with an understanding grin, "You must have got it down the Sunday throat."

This was a common remark in my case in those years. I cleared my throat, wiped my nose and my tears. I thought I'd try it again. To my utter embarrassment, I did it again, only a lesser attack.

By then, Howard and Yost realized that that must have been my first soda.

Howard said, "Next time I will give you a glass of milk with a few drops of Coke mixed in it.

About thirteen years later, I worked at a hospital as a conscientious objector. On my floor was a red machine with white letters that spelled *Coke*. One day I got brave enough when no one was around to try it again. I put a nickel in a slot, pulled a lever, and out rattled a bottle of Coke. I took a sip ever so small. No denying it was the same awful stuff. Much later I actually drank soda in a country where an American had better not drink the water.

Train Ride

Sometime in about the middle of the 1980s, we went to Wisconsin as a family to build a log home for my wife's sister and brother-in-law. We rode the train for the journey. While riding on the train, an announcement came on over the intercom.

"Your attention please! This is an announcement for Becky Miller to come to the cafe downstairs in the middle of the train and bring your sister with you. We have an important event for the two of you. When you get here, we will explain what it is that we would like for you to do. Thank you."

When they got there, this was what they said, "We have a big bag of small bags of M&Ms. We would like you two to pass them out to all that would like some. One pack per person."

They jumped at the opportunity and followed orders as instructed. When the job was done, they had plenty of M&Ms left to eat on the way and to share some with their cousins.

By the way, the conductor had seen Becky's name on her bonnet in the overhead luggage rack, and this was how he knew her name.

Store News

One of our workers in the store has been with us for around ten years, and whenever we get the opportunity, we try to outdo each other in all kinds of ways.

This one happened in an aisle in the store. I was working in the aisle, and a young mother was shopping in the same aisle. She had a baby buggy and was pushing it along with her shopping cart. In the buggy was a rather young baby. The abovementioned employee came through the same aisle that I was working in, as well as the woman with the baby buggy.

As the employee was walking by, he noticed the little baby in the buggy. He stopped briefly and talked to the baby. Then he came to me as he started to pass by. He suddenly stopped long enough to tell me that he made the baby smile.

Suddenly my brain clicked in, and I had a word for him. This is what I said to him: "So that baby smiled when she saw you. Well, that's nothing. When I first saw you, *I laughed out loud!*"

One hot summer evening

CHAPTER 6

❧

Hunting and Fishing

Fishing and Swimming Hole

Our neighbor, Yost Lehman, had a gravel and marl pit. We had permission to fish and swim in the gravel pit.

In the summertime, when supper was over and the chores were done, us boys would venture to the fishing and swimming hole with our homemade fishing equipment. The fish were not very big; nevertheless, they were fun to catch, and sometimes we caught a few big enough to eat. Because we caught them and cleaned them, somehow that seemed to make them taste extra good. Mom would fry them.

Now for the swimming part, that's a different story. This gravel pit was dug out with a crane with a scoop on the end of a few cables. The sides of the pond were fairly steep. We had no flat place to swim. The only defense we had were some planks we had in the water and some close to the water on the bank.

Our buzz word was always to be careful, be careful, the bank is steep, and the water is deep.

Nevertheless, a few years earlier the big boys were swimming in the same pond, and one of the boys slipped down the bank and went under the water. Some of the other boys got ahold of him and dragged him out of the water onto high ground. Needless to say, it was a big scare, yet not big enough for the next generation to take heed, and do not risk your life to do a little swimming.

Coon-Hunting

In our teenage years, my brother Henry and I loved to hunt coon. They were worth some money, yet I never heard of anyone getting rich on hunting coon.

At times our cousin, Menno Miller, would bring his coon hound over, and we would go back in the woods to hunt. The woodland had a lot of old trees on the twenty acres and half of the land was pasture. This made good homes for the coons in the hollow trees. The nearby cornfields, chicken houses, ducks, geese, fish, and such were all part of the coon's diets. They could riddle a patch of sweet corn. Therefore, they were considered a pest and a nuisance. For this reason, our parents had less opposition to us roaming around at night, chasing down coons ahead of the dog.

When Menno brought his coon hound, he'd find a fresh coon track and ran a coon all over the cornfield and through the woods. The coon would not go up a tree until he was tired or he thought the dog or dogs might catch up to him. Most of the time they would go up a tree, but once in a while they would go into their den inside of a hollow tree. If that happened, we were stuck. We would have to call it quits and either go home or find another one. It was tiring but very fun!

Coon-Hunting Dog

We had a border collie on the farm to help with the cattle and horses. He also became a good coon-hunting dog.

He was a silent trailer and could sneak up to an unalert coon, and then there was a fight. Somehow this dog would get them by the throat and would keep snapping and gripping his skin in front of his front legs. The dog would stretch the skin tighter and tighter until the coon went limp, and then we knew the fight was over.

Once in a while the dog would tree a coon. We would shoot it down. The coon would barely hit the ground, and the dog had it by the neck. and the struggle didn't last long.

Later on, brother Henry bought himself two young coon hounds. They became a great pair of dogs. He got married and sold his dogs to a man in Michigan. The man entered them in the Michigan State coon-hunting contest. They won first place and were featured in a coon-hunting journal.

Fishing Expedition

When I was about twelve or thirteen years old, some visitors from Ohio had close relatives with one of our neighbors. These visitors had a boy about a year older than I. They stayed at our neighbors for several weeks and went to our school while they were visiting.

We also were—that is, our parents—invited to their house for a noon meal. In the forenoon we played softball for a while and also after lunch. After a while we were finished with softball, and somebody said, "Why not go fishing?" All were in agreement.

In those days we didn't go to the nearest sports shop or the like for our fishing equipment. We made do with our own homemade equipment. Therefore, one of the boys that lived there went to the house and got several pins that the women used to pin their clothes on. He also acquired a small pliers and a roll of string that had been used to sow the feed sacks of chicken feed.

By the way, those feed sacks were made especially for the women. They made all kinds of cloth from the sacks, including our shirts. The women wore dresses made from them.

Now back to the fishing expedition. The pins were bent in the shape of a fishing hook. The string was tied on the pin. which had a head at the end of the pin. While the hook and line were assembled, several boys dug some worms, with that and a can of worms and a bucket to put our anticipated catch in. All that was still missing was the fishing poles. We took care of that when we came to the creek, which was at the back of the property about one half mile from the dwelling, we found a grove of willows and made them into fishing poles. Now with our strings tied to the poles and the worms on the hooks, we were ready to "go for it." This was not one of those fast-flowing creeks with deep pockets of water, mainly a four-inch-to-six-inch flow with pockets of maybe twelve inches to twenty inches. There is where the fish were. I don't recall a bucket full of fish, maybe a dozen, or at the most two dozen.

Nevertheless, this whole fish story is to bring out the results of this story many years later. Here it is!

Sometime in the mid-'eighties we received a letter from Ohio from some unknown friends. They were inquiring about the possibilities of a place to stay and the possibility of obtaining work for the summer. This man was a butcher by trade; in the summertime the business was slack.

We wrote back and informed them that those possibilities were fairly good, providing you were comfortable in staying in a small cabin close to our house:

> For the most part, it is occupied yet we do not have it promised to anyone. If you are interested in working with wood, we could include you into our workforce.

They accepted the offer and soon were working basically with me, erecting log homes. Therefore, we had a lot of communication. This arrangement went on for several years.

Then one time I mentioned about something I recalled from years in the past, mentioning that a family from Ohio came to visit one of our neighbors. They had a boy a little older than myself.

This boy went to school with us for, I believe, maybe a couple of weeks. Also, we played softball one afternoon at the neighbors where they stayed.

In the process of our conversation, he said I had an uncle in Indiana by the name of Elmer Schrock, and his wife was a sister to my mother.

One time long ago I did go with my parents to visit them, and I did go to school while we were there; and I did go along fishing, and we used bent straight pins for hooks and cotton fishline and corks for bobbers and young willow trees for poles, and last but not least, small nuts for sinkers.

That was all it took to settle the mystery. Yet we worked together for a couple of summers before we realized that we had played together, went to school together, and fished together.

The odds of this happening was the same odds as winning the state lottery.

Ora and Orpha Miller when they were on a trip to Hawaii in 2013.

Orpha Miller quilting in Libby, MT. for an auction.
The quilt auctioned off for $1,600.

Yoder cemetery in Shipshewana, Indiana.

Brother's short life changes many other lives for the better

Reaching Upward

By Lloyd Miller

It had been a hot July day in 1974. The fireworks we had watched from a distance the night before from our upstairs window kept us awake longer than usual. The three of us boys hung out the window in the dark exclaiming over the next display away to the northwest. Little did we know that it would be our last time together.

The next day found dad several miles off to the neighbors, putting up a field of hay on shares, as was common when there was more land than a farmer could take care of himself. On an adjoining farm that a neighbor had vacated, we had broken ground that year and put in late crops rather than see it go fallow again. This is where we three brothers were working the fields in the humid Indiana weather with our teams of horses, who constantly fought horseflies and gnats.

My brother, who was 9 and two years younger than I, had the job of lifting 50-pound bags of fertilizer onto a one-horse wagon. He would then deliver it to the back field a half mile away where my older brother was planting corn. My younger brother was light of weight and slight of build, but he made up for that in stamina.

On his way back up to the barn for another load that afternoon, my little brother stopped in the lane next to the field I was working in. He prepared to jump off the one horse wagon and hand me a jug of water. The flies caused his horse to jerk his head and take a small step. This slight movement caused my brother to almost lose his balance and fall off the back of the wagon where he was crouched with jug in hand. He gathered himself up and turned his attention to the horse, who had begun moving as if to run. Which he did!

As the wagon began bouncing, the reins fell away out of reach and no amount of "Whoas" would slow him down. I watched them disappear around the corner of the barn, gallop out the farm driveway, and make a 90-degree turn onto the road. As I ran up all I saw was my brother lying motionless on the pavement with the sounds of a runaway horse growing fainter in the distance. I knew if I picked him up it might be harmful, but by this time I was so overcome with shock that I picked him up anyway, calling his name and laying him in the shade on the lawn. There was no response. The pool of blood on the road indicated that some internal injury to his head caused his loss of consciousness.

When help finally arrived it was too late. The emergency crew nine miles away lost their way to the farm. My grandpa later said he heard them leave town going in the opposite direction. By the time they got there, an hour later, the policeman had decided to take him in himself.

The lack of professional response did not help our grief. Dad's heart was broken. This son was close to his heart; having suffered with him as a baby nine years earlier. At birth his trachea malfunctioned and the doctor had sent my parents home with no hope for healing or surgery for their third son. My parents were unwavering in their faith and commitment to care for him. They believed that God had greater plans than the doctor. And so it was; my brother was supernaturally healed from his breathing problem that was killing him and lived a very normal life up to the time of his tragic death.

A couple points about this story: The tidal wave of people that converged on our family from the hour of his death for a whole week following was indescribable. All the crops were brought in, the cows were milked, and everything was taken care of. Enough food was brought in for three days, not just for our family but for all of the many relatives as well. The big shed was cleaned and swept, benches set, and all the arrangements were made for the funeral and burial without us lifting a finger.

A second point is that my little brother's life was such a testimony that many people's lives were changed for the better. To this day there remains a fragrance of his life that cannot be denied.

And lastly, we know there's a multitude of people out there that have lost loved ones. Do we appreciate those who add value to our lives today? Are we prepared to face an eternity as suddenly as my brother? Does our love for one another match our appreciation should they be taken suddenly? Mine did not. I have lifelong regrets for not appreciating my brother when I had him, but then I was only 11 years old.

If it was you stepping into eternity, what fragrance would you leave? "Only one life 'twill soon be past. Only what's done for Christ will last."

Left to right, Becky, Leona, Joas, Lloyd, and
Elvie at Shipshewana, Indiana.

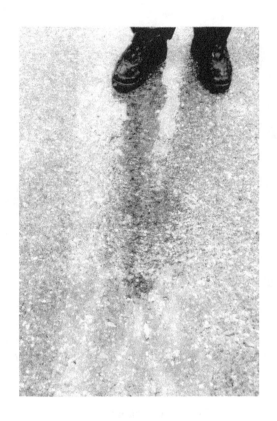

Vernon's rainbow.

Barn built by Ora's brother and around 100 others helped to build this in one day, 4 miles East of Shipshewana, Indiana, 1972–1975.

School house down the road from their house
in Shipshewana, Indiana in 1975.

The farm where Vernon lost his life in a horse
accident on the road to the left of the fence.

Home built by Ora and helpers in Shipshewana, Indiana in 1972.

CHAPTER 7

⚬∞⚬

Business Challenges

Lodge by the Lake

In the log-home business, as well as pretty much any business, a man can be put in some strange situations.

This is how this all came about. We came into an agreement with a group of Japanese businessmen who had a plan to build a rather large lodge by a lake—with the purpose of having a place of their own where they could send their head man and their spouses for short vacations.

Since they lived a long way from the job, they hired a young college-degreed man to oversee the construction. This seemed like a good idea on the surface. Yet in practicality, it caused almost instant chaos.

Now this—we'll call him—supervisor had no limits. First he bumped heads with the cement contractors, which made their work more difficult. This cost the company more money, and the owners had to pay the bill.

My aim is not to be too hard on this supervisor because he did do what he was hired to do, which was to supervise the job. That being said, where he and the contractor differed was in how the job should be accomplished. Their ideas were worlds apart. Efficiency never entered the supervisor's mind. He just wanted it done a certain way regardless of the time it took to do it.

When it was our turn to work with the supervisor, he seemed to be a really nice man. Yet we ran into the same problems that the other contractor experienced. When the first day was finished, we barely got half of the logs set that we normally would have got done. This was about one half of what we would have done if we had sat under a shade tree all day. This was the way it went doing the whole job.

When the time came to collect the last part of their payment, we didn't charge for the extra time spent because of the "supervisor."

At the end of the job, the businessmen gathered up all the leftover material and brought it all to us. It was a big truckload of stuff. I'll mention a few of the items: high-quality windows for our new house that we were planning to build, utility cabinets, and lumber and plumbing parts. We unloaded the whole job lot into our new "forty-by-eighty-foot storage shed that was nearly new. We picked out of the material for about a year and hauled the remainder to the dump.

The businessmen had told us that we were only contractors, and since we did not add onto the original price, it was only fair that we get the off falls. Now, that is a good lesson.

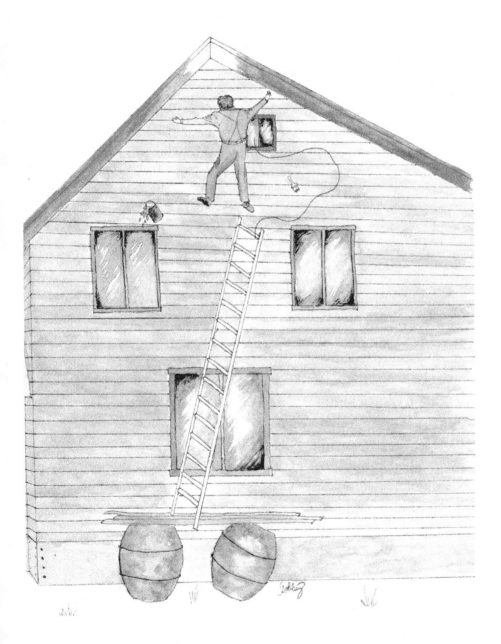

Learning the hard way

Trying to Paint with a 'Thirty-Two-Feet Ladder

Being in the construction business as a general carpenter has brought me into all kinds of challenging situations. Let me explain one.

We got a job to install a new roof on a house. This was on the last day as we were finishing up the job. I had one worker helping me by the name of Ivan, who now lives in Wisconsin. The owner of the property had just finished painting the house, except for one of the gable ends because his ladder was about four feet too short. So he asked me if I could paint it for him. I told him I would.

When the roof was all done, except the ridge cap, I said to Ivan, "Why don't you come down with me and help me set up the ladder to paint the gable end? Then I'll paint the gable end while you put the ridge cap on."

Ivan agreed, and we went to work.

Lo and behold, the ladder was five to six feet too short to reach the top. We were scratching our heads and looking around for a solution. We discovered a couple fifty-five-gallon oil drums. We brought them over and found a couple of planks. We sat the barrels on end and laid the planks on top of the barrels. Then we pushed the 'thirty-two-feet-extension ladder up and set the ladder on top of the planks. It seemed to be solid. The only thing missing was a rope tied to the ladder that ran through an open window with the end tied to the stove legs or anything solid and secure. Since it was setting pretty good, we felt good with our ingenuity. We relaxed and went to each of our projects.

With a can of paint in one hand and a paintbrush in the other, up the ladder I went. As I got to the top of the ladder and looked up, it looked to be a greater distance from this perspective than it had from the ground. Nevertheless, I was there now, and I had to make the best of my predicament. So I crept up the ladder, laid against the lap siding of the house, and pushed myself up inch by inch. I got on the top rung without too much hassle. There was an attic window on the right side of me, which helped somewhat to keep my stability and balance. Trying to dip my brush in the gallon pail that was half full of paint was not a small matter, to say the least.

I did manage to accomplish that feat and went about getting my brush with paint up to where it had to go. I had to reach up to the very peak of the gable, which was in the center of the peak. I was standing on the top rung and inching my way up about a foot and a half above my head. As I was making my last stretch with my arm, *alas!* I felt as if the roof raised away from the paintbrush. Instead, I was going down! I quickly pitched my brush and bucket and grabbed for the drip edge on top of the window. Of course, I couldn't hang on. Just that quickly, the bottom came up again, and I grabbed for it with the same results. In an instance the upstairs window flashed by me. I did get a chance to grab the windowsill. It was on a slant, and my fingers slipped off again. Next came so suddenly. I flew by three insulated electrical wires but chose to grab at the first-floor drip edge of the window, and this may have slowed me down just a bit, but it was all so fast I couldn't even think.

Before I could say, "Lord help me," I was laying on my back, looking up. I heard a *thump, thump* on the top of the roof. Lying there with my wind knocked out of me and still looking up, I saw a face popping out from the peak of the roof. It was Ivan, looking down and too scared to speak. He was out of breath from scampering across the peak of the house and then going down on his belly to look down to see what happened.

Still having the wind knocked out of me, I couldn't speak for a while. Ivan saw me move and saw that I was still conscious.

He hollered down, "Are you all right?"

I could somewhat squeak out something like this, "Y—ah—eh—e—c—h—b—i—n—all—right." I tried to say, "Yes I am all right."

Needless to say, the next day we had a 'forty-feet-extension ladder and finished the job with ease.

The moral of the story—never improvise. Do not try to do a job with a 'thirty-two-foot ladder when in fact it takes a 'forty-foot ladder!

Just Say No

Now I'll tell you a story of what a fellow can get himself into when you think you can't say *no!* That is just a two-letter word, yet looking back, it would have been much better to just say no. This would have saved me from taking on a volunteer job and going through a life-threatening experience.

Because I didn't say no, this person I was helping took me down to his basement and showed me a small crawl-through door that could be sealed up and opened into a water cistern. In earlier years these cisterns were quite common to catch rainwater from the roofs through eve-spouting, except this one was in the basement. The plaster was powdery and crumbling off. When I looked at it, I thought to myself, *If it were mine, I wouldn't think of repairing such a dilapidated has-been.*

Now, he kept saying that so and so wanted it fixed because they wanted rainwater to wash their clothes. Rainwater is so much better and softer on their cloth.

As a complete idiot and dummy, I said, "I suppose it could be done. However, it is going to be really dusty. Therefore, we would have to have a pressure water hose to wash it down on account of the dust."

There was no rental store within twenty miles that we knew of to rent a pressure washer. He suggested a bucket of water and a broom might do it. Since I had mentioned that it could be done, he took it to mean that I would do it. Right there I should have made it clear at that time. I should have said, "Unless you can come up with the proper equipment, I will not be able to do it."

There I was, pitying myself and knowing that I should have said, "I'm sorry, but my lungs are not good enough to handle the dust."

Even now I didn't realize that the worst that was coming was worse than I had expected it to be. As an uninformed dummy, I went inside the closed-up hole except for one small opening. As the concrete plaster came down, billows of dust filled the "six-by-eight-foot room. All of a sudden, with all the dust, the gas lantern I was using became dimmer and dimmer. This was on account of having no oxygen. I was getting light-headed and somewhat dizzy before I realized that I was about to pass out.

I don't recall just how it happened, but after that, I went upstairs and told my dilemma to the women. I had managed to get out, yet I didn't try to grab the lantern. Now a different scenario formed. The lantern was inside with the gas turned wide open, and gas was seeping out into the room. We were not daring enough to go down the stairs in case the gas ignited, and the worst that could happen is that the house blew up with us in it.

Someone would have to go down there with a lit lantern. Who knew what a cup full of gas turned into fumes would be capable of doing, and I wasn't about trying to find out.

So, besides the danger, I had gone to town and bought about $50.00 worth of materials and spent days doing the work. I could get all worked up about it. I could fume and get hot under the collar, but it's much better to grin and bear it. It's been a long time passed now.

Life is full of lessons. This is an unusual one that is hard to forget. I try not to recall it because it brings hurt. Just a reminder that I also make mistakes and do things at times that I need to beg forgiveness for.

Therefore, I have to do likewise to others. This reminds me of a proverb of my teacher. He quoted this: "Experience is the best teacher, but most times it comes too late to do any good."

Fire Station

Entering into a new year and into a new millennium, I was pondering what I have observed the past year and also the sixty some-odd years that I have memory of a lot of good has taken place on the positive side. A lot of improvements have been made in making life more pleasant and rewarding; I can think in the field of medical technology, communications, and transportation technology, and a host of other areas. These and many other areas have had its effect in changing the thinking of man, and if used properly and in the right principles and spirit, it can be a great benefit to mankind.

On the negative side, basically, I have worked with the public all my life, and I can honestly say I have enjoyed it. Of course, there have been some unfortunate and unpleasant happenings along the way. Yet even those can help us grow and mature. What, however, saddens me is the fact that thinking is changing. It is happening in our government and reaching down to all walks of life, and to some degree we are all affected.

Instead of using the biblical principle of doing unto others as you would have them do unto you, that principle is being weakened by the philosophy of getting all that you can get any way that you can. This can come in many ways; one way the government does it is by collecting more taxes to pay for some program or project that is supposed to help others. This might be well and good, but somehow the taxes seem to outweigh the benefits.

This now brings me into a present situation, where I was approached by a man that had two fire trucks. He asked us if we would consider erecting a building to house these trucks and in return have fire protection. Simple enough, I thought. We are roughly nine miles from the closest fire station. What could be better than having a fire station in our backyard? Everything seemed fine. We furnished the land and built the building. However, red flags started to go up as we approached the opening of the operation.

What I had in mind, they were telling me, won't work. My thought was that here was a fire station with two nice fire trucks. Whoever would like to be a part of it could be on their own free will. Nobody would be forced in, and nobody would be left out. In case of fire, all would be included if they asked for help even if they at the start thought they would rather not be a part of it. In other words, a mutual agreement upon the community that in case of fire, we would all pitch in and help each other.

We were being told our plan won't work; that we would have to become a local fire district being supported with tax dollars. This was where I drew the line. We have enough taxes as it is; we do not need to create more.

Whatever happened with the handshake and the mutual agreement among a local body or community where all agree upon a good cause to help each other for the benefit of all?

Instead, we all became suspicious of each other, fearing that through some mishap or human error, someone might sue us or get taken advantage of. It comes down to letting lawyers and insurance companies run our lives instead of all working together for a good cause and for the benefit of all mankind.

Building the Dam

Dear friends,

Greetings:

There are so many happenings that a person could relate to or write about. Some are embarrassing; others would not have much meaning to a stranger.

I'll let you decide if what I have in mind to write to you about interests you.

When we first bought this place here in Libby, I knew that it is not worth a lot unless we have a good source of water. This is the subject matter at the back end of our property. We have two creeks coming down from the mountain, and they become one creek running in a canyon in the middle of the property then running alongside of an open field in a dug ditch into another woodland and disappearing into the ground.

Therefore, the water never leaves the property unless, like the spring of the year, if we have a sudden snow meltdown or a downpour. We had to find a way to keep the water when it was needed for the crops. Therefore, we built a dam in the canyon. This caused an uproar a few years later after a heavy winter snow and a three-day rain, melting the snow really fast.

Even though we hired an engineer to design the structure, it failed because the water coming in was greater than the water going over the spillway. Therefore, the dam ran over, and it washed out, causing concern among some of the people that lived in the path of the overflow. Also washing the road out, leaving about a four-foot-deep by about eight-foot-wide gully in the blacktop.

This not only made big news in the county, it got to the national news and made news far and wide.

On account of that, I overheard in our store that there was going to be a water meeting at our store at 7:00 that evening. I thought to myself, *That's odd. A water meeting at our store, and we don't know about it.* Nevertheless, I thought maybe it was a rumor and didn't consider it very serious. However, I soon found out it was a mere fact and not a rumor.

A man walked into the store and exclaimed in a gruff voice, "*Where's the sheriff?*"

I answered and asked in a cool voice, trying not to shake, "Sheriff? Who needs a sheriff?"

"Who's going to *keep* order around *here?*" he exclaimed.

I said no more.

Soon others came, including three people from the Forest Service. They all carried suitcases of equipment. They got busy setting up a big screen and projector and a bunch of big maps. In the meantime, more people showed up; the dining room was pretty full.

Then the Forest Service guys took over. This is basically what they said: "We are from the Forest Service. We heard that there was going to be a meeting in regards to the dam on the Miller property. Since we have all the information on the property, including the dam, we came to present that information in case it isn't available otherwise."

Starting when it was government property and became into the hands of public owners through the Homestead Act, a lot of minor details were brought out—like when the first patch of ground was cleared and potatoes were planted to sell to the public.

Later logging companies bought or leased the land and built roads and a railroad with different spurs going in different directions. One log shoot was built where it was steep enough that the logs skidded down the hill. The shoot was made with planks in a V shape to keep the logs clean and going in the right direction.

Also included was a logging camp, including a cook shack and a dining room. Their running water never quit running. It ran on down the canyon and later into the ground; although some was diverted for crop use later.

Other aspects are still there to give a person a fairly good picture of how they lived. A good-sized hole in the ground is very telling of the concept of their restroom facilities. The dugout is still there, yet the building that covered the dugout either rotted away or has been moved off the dugout. A few moose heads and bones are still lying around, telling us of their meat supply.

Now getting back to the water meeting. The Forest Service explained many details, then they came to the time the Millers bought the property, showing every detail—the process of the transaction etc. Then they got out a copy of the letter written by yours truly, Ora Miller, asking and inquiring in regards to getting a permit to build a dam in the canyon of the property.

After reading the letter, he had another letter written by the state department in answer to the request for a permit. This is what that letter said. The answer—they wrote something like this:

> Regarding the request for a permit to build a dam. This is what the law says. If the water or creek that runs into your property is determined to be an intermediate stream, you do not need a permit to build a dam. Again the creek that runs into your property is determined as an intermediate stream therefore you do not need a permit to build a dam.

Now, the man that came in earlier and asked, "Where's the sheriff," got up and exclaimed, "I have been told that the dam was put in illegally!" Then as he walked for the door, he said this, "This is the biggest railroading attempt I've seen in all my *life*!"

Much more could be added in regards to the dam and water supply. Yet I believe the main story has been covered to the best of my knowledge. Therefore, "All is well that ends well."

The Woodcutting Business

Recently I had a conversation with a customer in the store. His wife was shopping, and he was sort of meandering around the store, looking things over, when we met in the isle. I greeted him and made the remark that I should probably know him. He returned the greeting and introduced himself. Then we had some light conversation, which soon turned into more serious talk, also that he had worked on our ranch, working with an excavating crew.

One thing led to another. He talked about how the young generation doesn't want to work and feel somehow that people that already have a start in life owe them a free ride or a living without working.

Giving an example of his own family, a grandson came to him, asking for a job. He said he would hire him and help him get started in life. He started out okay yet soon was coming to work late and being low in energy on account of not enough sleep, staying up late playing video games and watching movies etc. After about a month or so, he decided it was just too much to have to be at a place of work at a given time. He was accustomed to being his own boss and doing what he wanted to do and when he wanted to do it.

Therefore, he mustered up enough courage to tell his boss, which was his grandfather, that he wants to quit and go into the woodcutting and selling business. As a wise grandfather, he asked him if he had money saved up to get into the woodcutting business.

He had to admit that he didn't. Well, he admonished him that he should at least work long enough and save his money to buy a truck and chainsaw to get started. He also realized that he didn't like the work, and if he didn't like the work, there is no need to force him into something that he dislikes. Therefore, he told him, "I'll even go a step forward to get you started. I'll buy you a truck and chainsaw to get you started.

"This is the deal: when you sell a load of wood, you keep what you need for your expenses. The balance you pay on the truck and saw. I will charge no interest, just pay me for what it cost me. However, if somehow after one year, you can't pay a good part of the money that you owe, I will have to take the truck back."

You guessed it. After a year was up, he had paid zero down and ran the truck with disrespect so that the value was almost gone.

Now the boy is back playing video games and watching movies and listening to rock and roll and rap to dull his mind and keep him from being bored to the extent of keeping him sane enough and keeping him from losing his mind.

Think of this: there are statistics out that found that there are five million young folks in the United States from the ages of sixteen to twenty-six that have no job and/or do not go to school. Basically, they spend most of their time with electronics, movies, and listening to rock and roll and rap.

These young people, instead of being beneficial to society, being full of energy, with a sharp mind, in the prime of their life, have become a drag on society and are helping to bring this country down. *Who is to blame?*

Work Ethic

We hear a lot in regards to work ethic. I hear many elder people complain how hard it is to hire younger people to be responsible workers. All they think about is how much you pay. What about paid vacation and time off for events etc.

This basically is how things were done on the farm:

From birth until I was ten years old, my folks had a fifty-acre farm. They milked from six to eight cows; had about the same amount of cows. They had two litters of piglets a year of from seven to twelve per litter. They would have their pigs in the fall and again in the spring in individual portable huts. Also, we had about 250 chicks. When the roosters were from four to five pounds, we would catch them in the evening and put them in chicken crates made especially for this purpose—to be butchered the next day.

I will mention here that wintertime was butcher time. The size of the families usually determined the number of animals that were butchered, usually one beef and from two to eight hogs weighing around 250 each. Someone in the neighborhood always had butcher tools. These tools or equipment were taken from place to place.

Before we went to school, us children went along; everyone had such good food. I'll never forget how good those mashed potatoes and chicken gravy tasted from one of those little spoons with those bent handles, where our little hands had more grip and more control.

After we were married, we never missed butchering days until we moved to Montana. We did take our butchering tools along and also did some butchering. Yet there were few people that had livestock. Everybody got their meat out of the woods, and they were mostly butchered one at a time.

More on Work Ethic

Regarding work ethics. In the culture I grew up in, we were part of a clan that had a cause and had skin in the matter.

Whereas in today's culture there is no gain in helping each other out. The government is there to take care of our needs.

For instance, they will pay the parents to support them for all their needs. That is, until they are twenty-six years old.

Therefore, there is no need to look for a job. To look at it another way, they are living the "life of Riley". It would do away with the "free life" and add on misery to their life if they had to fend for themselves.

Now by the time they reach the age of twenty-six, they would now have to fend for themselves. First of all, who would hire a twenty-six-year-old that hasn't worked a lick in their lives?

I could go on and on. Enough said!

Even More About Work Ethic

The difference in today's world culture in comparison is this. Everyone had skin in our coming and going in whatever we did. During the day we all joined together in helping each other in whatever needed to be done.

After the work was done and the evening meal was over, which we called supper, we most always had time to play ball or kick the can.

Elsewhere I mentioned my dad hired me out to drive the team for our neighbor's spray business. For that he paid Dad $1.00 per day. I felt honored to help out and contribute to the cause.

The next two years my brother Ervin and I went with dad with a stationary baler, baling straw stacks and hay every day that the sun shined. One of us threaded the wire, and the other tied the wires as they came through a slotted wood block dividing the bales.

Later in the spring of 1945 we moved to a 154-acre farm. One of my parent's good friends bought forty acres of the land for pasture for his cattle. This helped my parents going from 50 acres to 154 acres. They agreed that he could have it for five years, at which time my dad could buy it back if he wished. I was assigned to help his bigger and older son to fence off the forty-acre track.

As the years rolled by, my dad had the extra help. People came to Dad and asked for help. When I was fourteen a neighbor that lived about two and a half miles from us asked for one of the boys with a team and wagon to help haul or thrash clover hay for seed.

That is the second cutting. Clover was worth more for seed than to put it in the barn for hay. My dad sent me, since the clover hay was light and had to be loaded with a fork by hand. There were three other wagons, and I believe we each loaded one load in the forenoon and two in the afternoon.

When it was time to leave, the owner gave me $7.00. I whistled all the way home. I could not wait to give my dad the $7.00. It never dawned on me that somehow the $7.00 was mine. I gladly gave it for the cause.

This example might help explain to the ones that don't know why today's young folks don't know how to work.

The motto of the story—if a person is spoiled for twenty-six years, it will take that person another twenty-six years to get unspoiled, and by then it is a little late in life to change the thinking.

What the examples should portray is all about what Christ taught—that is, to live a selfless life not for self but for others. If that is practiced, do not do it for the following reasons—that is, if you will look out for others and by that, help a cause. Do it not because it will also help you.

What is meant by that is, if a person does something that will bring self-benefit, there is no true gain in that. Whereas, if a person does a deed that is meant only for the sake of the other person, that is an unselfish and true deed.

In the German translation, Jesus said this, "*Liebe deinen nächsten als dich selbst.*" That is to say, "Love the one close to you." As you love yourself, never make a glow of self.

If a person does that, that very thought pattern will grow on others unto a community. If that is practiced in a community, it will grow unto other communities and on and on.

D8 Caterpillar

There was a big sawmill in the town of Libby that was still operating when we moved in the area. They had a big retail lumberyard on the premises where we bought a lot of lumber for our log-home business.

History has it that around the turn of the century in the 1800s and 1900s, it was the largest sawmill west of the Mississippi. By the way, the buzz was out among the crowd that it gets hot. Therefore, we bought for $14,000. Now we had a machine worth maybe between $40,000 to $50,000, costing us $15,500 and proving this proverb to be true, "No venture, no gain." Nevertheless, win a few, lose a few is also true. Here is an example where discernment helps.

Now they were selling the business because the Forest Service shut down the timber sales on account of the environmentalists, which, in turn, came up with ideas of how they could challenge the Forest Service which was the government. In the process, shut down the forests!

Therefore, they did not have enough logs to keep running. So this is what happened. They had a big sale and sold all their property consisting of four hundred acres and some huge buildings, along with all their equipment, at public auction. Everything was sold "as is." They had a D8 caterpillar that we figured we could use. Therefore, we went and inquired and looked at the cat and asked the ones that knew all about the machine.

It was a really old machine and looked like it had its day; yet they—that is, the mechanics—showed us the parts bill where they overhauled the whole undercarriage and the final drive etc. However, they also told us it gets hot if it is used hard.

They also told us it could be as little as a leaking head valve. However, it could also mean it might need a new engine. Without labor, that could run from $10,000 to $15,000, plus labor. They showed us the parts bill for what it cost them, which was $26.000.

We really needed a crawler of good size. Decided to bid on it up to $20,000 and take a chance even if we had to put in a new or used motor or engine.

We got tremendously blessed. It got hot on account of a leaky head gasket, costing $1,500 and maybe $100 for part and the remainder for labor. We have used it a lot for twenty-five years and has been the best buy in machinery that we ever bought.

I wrote all this to say what a friend said that worked with us for several years. He stopped by recently with his family to reconnect and visit. He asked about the cat.

It starts and runs like a clock. To which he replied, "That was Elvie's first racecar," noting that when he ran it, he thought it had only one gear that was "high gear!"

Sharing Scriptures

CHAPTER 8

❧

Missionary Service

Missionary Experiences

Now I am going to tell you about my missionary experiences. I always thought it would be nice to go abroad and help some poor people and help spread the message of Jesus Christ.

My desire became a reality when I learned that an agriculture officer and also a minister was looking for someone or persons to go with him on a mission to a communist country on a government program to promote a connection of good will toward this country. We were on a program to teach them how to raise chickens. Also, on the side we could teach them of Jesus Christ and the plan of salvation. We were to fly to New York to meet there and fly together after that. It was planned that if one or the other somehow missed a flight and didn't make the connection, whoever was there was to go as planned, and whoever missed the flight was to somehow follow later. As fate would have it, when I got there, the other guy didn't show up. Therefore, I was on my way to the other side of the world all by myself. My first stop was Istanbul, Turkey, where there was a day layover before going the flight to the city of Uzbekistan.

There I was fortunate enough to meet my interpreter, and he took me to the place where we were to stay. A day later my partner-to-be and boss showed up.

The first day our chauffeur took us to our headquarters. Now for a few small details. This was a large communist-built structure. It was very busy and built for efficiency: two stories, a stairway in the center, with hallways down the center and offices on both sides.

There was one bathroom in the building. It was conveniently placed by the stairway, making it convenient for both floors. There was no door to the bathroom. There were somewhere between twenty and thirty open stalls. There were no toilet stools, only a gutter about ten to twelve inches wide and about three to four feet long. I couldn't tell how deep it was because I couldn't see the bottom. I suppose it could have been about six inches deep. The weather was warm, and you can guess the rest.

I was free to go while the boss had a few more things to finish. So the interpreter and I went out to the car. I was ready for fresh air. While we were waiting in the car, the Muslims were giving their evening prayer from a loudspeaker somewhere not too far from us. So our conversation turned to the Muslims. I soon learned that he wanted nothing to do with their religion.

Now, I thought this is a perfect opportunity to tell him about Jesus. So I asked him if he knew about Jesus.

He quickly and very emphatically replied, "I do not know about a Jesus, and I do not care to hear about Jesus. I have heard about all the religion that I care to hear, and I am fed up with it, and I don't want to hear anymore. End of conversation."

I was dumbstruck! Here I was on the other side of the world. I came basically to tell people about Jesus that maybe never heard of him. Now if my interpreter wasn't willing to hear about Jesus, I sure couldn't tell anyone else about him without going through him.

This is basically what was our purpose and schedule. It was something like this. Plans for us were to visit, I believe, twelve districts. However, being we were one day late, we missed one meeting. This was how the meeting went. Each day we had a certain district meeting at a conference room where from thirty to fifty people showed up.

The questions we were basically answering were to be about raising and taking care of chickens, mainly laying hens. It wasn't that they were unfamiliar with laying hens. A number of people raised a few chickens with setting hens. A dozen hens and a rooster would be about max for one family. More would deplete the feed supply. They basically were loose and ran around the neighborhood, picking up whatever they could find and, in the process, laid a few eggs.

How to raise chickens in any amount above a dozen was outside of their capacity of thinking. They lived on government property existing of a glorified shelter, calling it their home. Also, they had about one half to one acre of land for their own purpose. On that small acreage, it was amazing how much food they could produce.

Yet right alongside these small parcels was hundreds of acres lying bare. Not even weeds looked hardy. Only scrubby bushes grew on the unfarmed land. The only thing that still existed of these collective farms was the small patches that had been given to them to use only, not to own, in the beginning of this collective farm venture.

I remember as a growing boy, they were building the collective farms. I well remember how they were boasting how they were going to surpass the United States and the world in food production. All I can say to that is, it takes more than boasting to make it happen.

This is my take on the matter. Well, okay. So be it. Here I am twelve thousand miles from home. As the saying goes, if you are dealt a lemon, make lemonade. So I'll just make the best of it. Maybe I can at least teach some poor peasants how to raise chickens. To say the least, I was so thoroughly disappointed.

Now something interesting happened as we came to the end of our mission and were getting ready to leave. I noticed some of the secretaries and others were talking about us, and they were saying that there was just something about us that made them curious. So they asked me what beliefs I had. I explained to them that I held strong to the teachings of Jesus Christ, and that gave us strength, and if we had faith in him, we did not need to worry.

As it came about, my interpreter was listening. He became interested and asked if I had a Bible that he could have. I told him I had a couple versions. He gladly took the Bibles and literature that I had. So they say God works in mysterious ways, and this was one of those times. It seems that no words needed to be said, but setting an example was the best way to bring Jesus to others.

Purpose of the Ministry

This is a legitimate question. Who should I join and with? What group should I associate with in order to come into the fullness of God and the spirit in the body of Christ? The answer is so simple most people stumble over it in order to find it. God has preordained you to be one with himself. Over time he has shaped and molded you as you yielded to his calling and the working of the spirit, chastised and disciplined you for that purpose he has for you. Again, that ultimate purpose is to mold you to become one for himself.

Therefore, the purpose of the ministry is exactly that—to direct people to him by way of the cross. May the lamb that was slain receive the reward of his suffering. Fulfilling his purpose through faith is a way he is being rewarded for his suffering.

Any ministry that succeeds, knowingly or otherwise, to bring its member or the body in union with the ministry instead of the union with the son fails in its purpose.

Paul writes to the Ephesians, explaining what Christ did and for what purpose. First he set the ministry in order, then he explained the purpose of it—for the perfecting of the saints, for the work of the ministry, for the edifying of the body of Christ "till we all come in the unity of the faith." (4–13) The German translation says it something like this, "Till we all come to believe and acknowledge the Son of God and becoming a man of fulfillment."

Coming into fulfillment is not necessarily doing something. It is becoming something by believing and being, thereby coming into fulfillment. It happens by renewing our minds and being regenerated. The end result of that is man of fulfillment, man meaning human being man or woman. Paul says, "By grace are you saved through faith, not works, lest anyone should boast."

CHAPTER 9

⊸≋⊹

Libby Happenings

Book Inspiration

Bruce gave me a daily devotional, *My Utmost for His Highest* by Oswalt Chambers.

I would like to quote a full page of this inspiring book. However, since it is copy written, I will only quote two sentences from page 194. The message is being taken from Eph. 4–13.

This is Oswald's message taken from that verse:

> The church ceases to be a spiritual society when it is on the lookout for the development of its own organization. It will be a big humiliation to realize that I have not been concerned about realizing Jesus Christ, but only about realizing what He has done for me.

This Bible verse and Oswald's admonishment helped me to inspire my thoughts regarding the writing of this book.

Montana

When we moved to Montana, we had to shift some gears. I have made the remark, when asked how Montana compares with living in the east, when you are in Rome, you do as the Romans. Of course, the challenges are different; nevertheless, it is not about the challenges that make it different. It is all in what you do with those challenges.

No matter where we live or what we do, God's principles never change. His word teaches much about being overcomers. God helps us through as we overcome.

Secretary

I'm planning to write about having a secretary. Some might think, that surely would be a boring story. Maybe so, yet I'm going to give my two cents' worth.

As I was growing up, Farm Beaura, a feed-mill business, had calendars which had pockets where the numbers were, where we inserted all our sales slips etc. for the month. At the end of the month, they were taken off and stored in a box. In our house these boxes were stored under the bed.

When we got married, we did the same for many years. If perhaps you wanted to check on something, in those days word of mouth was considered all that was needed.

For example, one of the first years we were married we raised a few litters of pigs. As customary, we put an ad in the local paper: Weaner Pigs for Sale. A farmer came by which I had never met. He told me he would take them and bring his truck on such-and-such day. I told him that would be fine.

Then he asked me if he should pay some money to hold them for him.

I said, "No, I'll hold them for you."

When he came to pick them up, he paid as promised. Then he said this, "When I was a younger man, I stopped at a farmer's house that had a 'Farm for Sale' sign up."

He knew the farmer well, and he asked him, "How much do you want for your farm?"

He replied, "I want such and such for the farm."

Then this farmer studied a bit, then he said, "I'll take it."

The farmer was sitting on the front porch on a rocking chair with a cane in his hand.

When he heard him say, "I'll take it," he stumped his cane on the porch floor twice and exclaimed, "*Sold!*"

Then he asked him, "Do you want some money to hold it for me?"

He again stumped his cane on the floor and repeated his former words, "*I sold this farm!*"

Today a person has to be careful. There are too many people out there that will take advantage of people if you give them a chance. Over the years we have dealt with people that were looking for ways to take advantage of others.

Here is where a good bookkeeper or secretary can make a big difference.

This is the way it started. One Sunday evening a young couple came into our community and were looking for a place to stay. They had three children somewhere between two and eight. We gave them a place to stay at our house for the night.

As it turned out, they stayed around for some time. Since we were in the log-home business, he said he knew of a doctor or two that were looking to have a log home built for them.

As it turned out, one of the doctors called and asked me if I would consider coming to his place and come up with a plan for his home. That was what I did, and we built the log home for him.

This guy that told me about the house never helped or spent any time with him in selling or building. Yet he wanted 10 percent of the money that I received. He wanted cash, so we gave him cash. We received $52,500. Therefore, we paid him $5,250. Therefore, I wanted his handwriting on the bill that he was to give me for proof of him receiving the same. I handed the receipt book to him and asked him to put the date and the amount on the receipt and sign it for us.

Now, I thought it sort of weird that he didn't use the whole sheet; instead, he wrote across the corner, and then he tore that part off and handed me a triangle piece of paper.

I felt like making him rewrite it, yet I didn't want to rock the boat, and I took the piece of paper and stuffed that piece of paper among the many other much-bigger sheets, however much less meaningful.

I took him to be the simpleton that he was and forgot the "rest of the story."

This is "that story." About five years later a stranger came to our place we were working at the mill. He told me with a tremendous amount of certainty and determination he showed me a piece of paper that he got from this man, and he told me in no uncertain terms that he came to collect the money, and he wanted it now.

I told him, "Not so fast. I'm going to the house and find the receipt that he signed to get the money."

Now, this is what I believe happened. This man that signed the triangle piece of paper thought surely by now I could not come up with such a small piece of paper after five years. What he didn't know was who he was dealing with. This was why I had a secretary that kept track of every detail no matter how small.

To say that when we—my wife and secretary as well—showed the piece of paper with the exact amount and his signature as well; to say that this man was shocked out of his wits is describing it mildly.

He didn't say a word and made a beeline for the door, and I haven't seen him since.

Fasting

When we first moved to Libby in the 'nineties, at times we'd go on fasts. This was on a somewhat-regular basis. One time a younger brother and I decided to go on a water fast for a week. With two of us, it was easier to stay on it as we could encourage each other. I had learned from the past that the third and fourth day were the hardest. Once you got past the fourth day, you had the battle pretty much won, as it became easier after the fourth day.

We both had completed the seven days as we had agreed upon. Yet I was feeling good, and I decided to go on another day. Then on the morning of the eighth day, as I woke up, I felt a sensation coming into my head, entering at the top of my head. This sensation slowly but steadily flowed down through my head, filling every part of my head like my ears and nose were completely filled with the sensation.

This sensation kept going down through my body, filling my legs, feet, and the very tips of my toes. Then it slowly went away. Yet I was completely relaxed. Feeling graciously uplifted, all I could think was, *How wonderfully marvelous.* Now looking back, and I having nothing to boast about, all I can say is maybe because I am such a stubborn person the Holy Spirit had to literally show me the filling of the Holy Ghost in order to make me believe in him. Whatever the reason, to this day I cannot quit being thankful for what he showed me.

No chicken with a belly ache

Fourteen-Year-Old

About the middle of August of 1992 son Elvie, age twenty-two, and our youngest son, Joas, age twelve, came with us—myself and three young men from Ohio who heard we had bought a ranch in the Libby area in Montana. One of those boys had brought a fourteen-year-old boy along. His dad wanted to send him along. This is the advice he gave to this young man that he put in his care.

Now, the young boy's dad was a minister in his church. He had a title of a bishop or something similar. He was a full-time preacher or whatever, stating that he never had time to work with his son and couldn't teach him how to work. Therefore, he thought this should be a good opportunity to send him along with this young man, and he could work with him and teach him the responsibilities of life and how to work.

This is what the dad of this young boy said: "I am giving you full authority of my son to teach him and to discipline him. Do whatever you think is helpful to develop him in making him an upright and responsible person to his God and to his fellow man."

The following statement is my own opinion: Trying to teach a fourteen-year-old the facts of life and how to work when he thought carrying the trash out or making his bed was almost too much for a fourteen-year-old.

Now, as you might imagine, there were quite a few challenges. The first one that I was involved with was this. I was thinking what the boys might do instead of uselessly playing around, throwing rocks and such.

Now, basically, this young man was a fine, young man. All that he yet needed (like all of us) was some basic teaching. I called the boys to me, and this was what I said, "Here is a stack of rebar, about forty pieces, twenty feet long. This is what I want you to do.

"Joas, you take a hold of the rebar right here like this, about two or three feet from the end, and your friend Tom can take the other end and carry them over there where that stake is that I just drove in. This will give you a good appetite. You know what great meals Bruce always makes. You will have plenty of time to move them before Bruce has our meal ready. I suppose he will leave shortly to get the meal started."

Then there arose a crisis after carrying about a half dozen or so. This young man got a severe tummy ache. He could hardly stand up straight. It came on rather quickly. He was fine about fifteen minutes ago when they were throwing rocks. I was pondering what to do. Bruce came quickly to my rescue.

He said, "I'll take care of the matter."

He told Tom, "Come over here and sit by this tree in the shade. It might make you feel better."

I knew Bruce had something up his sleeve. Therefore, I didn't say a word. I asked Joas if he thought it might be too much to do it himself.

"No, I can just take hold of one end and drag them over," he said.

It was about forty or fifty feet. He had just finished, and we all went a half mile down the lane to where Bruce was just finished with the meal.

"I see Tom didn't get any worse. At least he is up and walking around," Bruce declared.

Someone said, "That shade tree sure was a good thing. He seemed to get better fast and got up quickly when I asked him if he is good enough to go along with us."

It smelled really good going toward the house. All gathered around the table, asked God to bless the food, and thanked him for being our Lord and Savior.

Now there was no plate for Tom's setting, only a soup spoon. Nevertheless, Tom reached in for a piece of chicken.

Bruce stopped him as he placed a bowl of soup in front of him as he said, "*No! No!* You cannot have chicken with a belly-ache. I made soup for you!"

He wanted to make a big scene and started to choke up when Bruce quickly, very sternly told him, "Today you are sitting at my table, and I have rules. Just be content and eat your soup."

This probably was a rare instance and very likely the first time in his life that he got stopped in his tracks and didn't get his own way.

Now I do not care to bring out all this boy's faults, yet lessons can be learned by bringing things to light when any young person is left to themselves. The Bible teaches to train up a child in the way he should go. When he is old, he will not depart from it. Furthermore, by neglect or otherwise, you can *keep* training out of a boy. However, it would be hard to *take* training out of a boy.

These three young men volunteered to come to Libby and help us with building and to help get established in this new venture. This proved out to be a great blessing for us, which we will never forget. Three young men knew how to work. Also being grounded in faith, they took life seriously, first spiritually as well as physically.

There was another problem that Bruce had with this young lad. He was very picky with his food. He only liked certain foods. When he didn't take what he thought he didn't like, he just passed it by and didn't take any. One day Bruce served green beans. He didn't want to take any. Then Bruce himself dipped him a small portion of beans and advised that he could surely eat a small portion. He took a small bite and started to gag and made a scene. Bruce firmly told him to quit gagging and eat the rest of his beans.

To say that Bruce's statement infuriated him is being very generous. Tom got red in his face, and as he took a small bite again, he started to gag and spit out the beans. One of the other boys sitting next to him had enough. He got out of his chair, took his belt off, and jerked this lad out of his chair.

"We've seen enough of your antics, and you are under a new set of conduct. We know these are good beans! You have a choice. You can now sit down and eat them without one gag, or you are still free to choose not to eat them. With that choice, you will get a whipping of your life with this belt! One you will not soon forget!"

With that, he sat down and ate all his beans without a sound and as if they were delicious. I have to say, there were no more eating problems after the episode.

Letters from Tom and His Dad

A few months after the boys left and Tom went along home, we received a letter from Tom's dad and one from Tom as well.

This letter had all kinds of praises and thanking us for giving Tom a home and the wonderful teaching that Tom received. Even Tom thanked us for teaching him regarding work ethics etc.

That being said, I believe Tom and the other three boys taught myself and two of my own boys as much as they learned from us. It did all of us good to see someone that had been left to himself without proper teaching.

Seeing his own faults and admitting the same and turning his life around, I believe all of us saw what Tom had to go through because he never really had to listen to anyone; thereby running his own course.

I do believe Bruce took his responsibilities seriously, and the other two boys stood with him. That is what changed him—in the natural.

Having said that, the real test is or was still to be determined. Following Christ and denying himself and taking up his cross and following him also has to take place, as well as taking his yoke upon himself and leaning of him. That will or was the real test. That goes for all of us; all of the above because it is all about Christ and his suffering for us. Rev. 5–12 says, "Worthy is the lamb that was slain to receive power, and riches, and wisdom, and strength, and honor, and glory, and blessing."

It follows that all of the above is all because of Christ and what he did for all of us. Therefore, he has to receive all the glory. Amen. That being said, we all will have to suffer for Christ's sake and lose it all for him as he did for us.

More History of Libby Property

A little more history regarding our property here in Libby. Our children and my wife, Orpha, and I bought this property in July 1992, consisting of 830 acres, as I stated earlier. Elvie, twenty-two, Joas, twelve, and three boys from Ohio built a forty-by-eighty log structure consisting of living quarters, a dining room, living room and kitchen combination, three bedrooms, and a bath.

In the spring of '94 we moved from that dwelling into our home close by. Robert Mast and his family then moved into this dwelling. A year later they moved into their new home a half mile away on the property. We then took the partitions out of the building and made it into a store. A few years later, we added a "twelve-by-thirty-six-foot addition for a cooler and freezer. A few years later we added a "thirty-two by thirty for a store and storage room. Later a "thirty-two by fifty was added.

Then in spring 2017 the boys added another, roughly eight thousand square feet. This was basically enclosed by the fall of that year. The boys had planned to finish the interior during the winter of that year. Yet before they got started, they got some company coming in some fancy and high-class duds. They asked Elvie where the permits were. He didn't know. He advised them that we hand the plans to the county planners. Then sometime later they told all was okay and they could commence to build, and this is as far as we got. We are planning to finish the building in the winter.

They advised Elvie that "you have to go through the state as well. You may not do any more work until we give you the permits." They put "stop work" orders up! The permits didn't come until March of the next year. By then, the boys had committed on home projects, and the right kind of help was not available.

Hindsight is 20-20. Yet this maybe is what we should have done. We heard by the "gossip vine" that help is available in Scotland. Here is an example of the gossip. Two brothers were out of work, searching high and low. Someone told them there was work in America.

The brothers got all excited and made preparations to go to America. Then someone advised them something like this: if only one went and checked it out. If he didn't find any work, he would just come back. That way you would only lose one half of the money. It sounded like sound advice. This is what he wrote back to his brother. This is what he wrote: Come over right away. There is a lot of work here. I already have a job for us. All we have to do is carry *mud* and *bricks* up a ten-story building. There is a guy up there that does all the work!

Repent for Your Soul

After living in Rexford for seventeen years, we bought an 830-acre ranch, ten miles south of Libby. Soon after we acquired the ranch is when the three boys from the east came to visit Rexford. Learning of our decision to move to Libby, they offered to come out to Libby and help us build. Some of the buildings included a "forty-by-eighty-foot building, of which we finished off one end for the purpose of living quarters, and also a "forty-by-eighty-foot storage shed; also a "forty-by-eighty-foot cement slab for the purpose of erecting log homes since that was our occupation in Rexford for about fourteen years. Then there were two cabins, plus a central bath and wash cabin built to accommodate the cabins.

The basement was also poured for our personal dwelling, which we didn't build until the next spring. Our son Elvie and I, plus the three boys from the east, built the abovementioned structures.

We started the project in the middle of August and moved in the building, which is now the store, October 9. There was a farmhouse on the property about a half mile down the lane from the job sight and a path through the hayfield where we ate and spent the night. One evening, when we were just finishing dinner, we noticed a vehicle at the sight where we were working on a building.

Bruce quickly turned to me and said, "Let's go see what's going on."

As he sped down through the field, one of the Mennonite boys ran for his van. I went with him. It was just getting dark. We drove down without lights. When we got close, we saw two men carrying the generator. They were ready to lift it into the back of their van.

All of a sudden they noticed us. We saw them dropping the generator and running toward their station wagon; the back door was wide open. The wheels were spinning and throwing gravel as they got to the open gate just ahead of us. When they got on the pavement, they took off like a scared rabbit. In the process, a big cooler slid out the back door of their van. We pushed it down the road a little, then it went under the van we were in. Then all of a sudden the Styrofoam cooler started to smoke, sending billows of smoke coming out from under the van. In the process, Bruce had to stop and back up. By the time the hot pursuit was all but over, they were way down the road. We couldn't catch up with them, so we turned around and headed back before we lost control and caused a wreck. We decided to call our pursuit over.

The cooler was still smoking and about burned up. Beer bottles were scattered all over the road and in the ditch. On our way back, we checked the building site and found the transit gone.

That night there was a prayer meeting on for these two men with enthusiasm. Not so much that we would get our transit back even though it cost somewhere between $1,000 and $1,500. The most emphasis was on the men on repenting and bringing the transit back for the sake of their soul.

The next morning when we were eating breakfast, a station wagon came down the lane and stopped by our house. I went out to meet them. They came over to where I was standing with their heads hanging low.

They said, "They are the ones stealing your stuff, and they are prepared to give themselves up and go to jail."

I quickly invited them into the house and introduced them to the ones at the table, telling them, "Basically, since you came to make it right and repented, there is no way we would require you to take it to the law. For your sake, we are here to accept your apology and forgive you, and Christ can set you free."

CHAPTER 10

❦

Orpha and I, Beginning

Courtship of My Wife

One of the oldest grandchildren wanted me to write about our courtship years. This episode took place in the first year of my civil service in a hospital at the north end of Fort Wayne, Indiana. The first year of my service I had Sunday off every two weeks, coming home too late to go anywhere.

To expound a little regarding my time off from my civil service in the hospital near Fort Wayne, Indiana, I got off work at three thirty. By the time I got home it was around 6:00. Therefore, the only real time I had to go anyplace was after church the next day. That was the reason to check on my hopeful future girlfriend and maybe a living companion on a late Sunday afternoon.

We were "going to church" the next day, as we used to call it. Later I realized we do not go to church; "we are the church." Anyway, we'll leave that as it may be for now.

At any rate, I had Orpha on my mind and decided to take a venture and go and see her. At least I could find out if she might be at home. I don't recall who answered the door.

I was heartily invited to come on in; she is here. When Orpha heard that I was here, she welcomed me in and asked me if I had supper.

I replied, "I didn't come for supper. Please don't bother about me. I came to see if perhaps you might want to go to the singing or maybe just visit."

Orpha talked to her dad about our conversation. He told her, "Why don't you ask him to stay, and we can visit a while here in the living room. If you want some private time alone, you can have that too."

I replied, "That would be perfect!"

I have told Orpha many times since "that it was the best date in all my life."

This was the beginning of our serious thoughts about our future life together. Within about four months, we were committed to each other in regards to a marriage.

After that commitment on January 17, 1956, it took exactly one year and three days before it became a reality.

German School

The down side of writing your memoirs is the fact that if you write your memoirs, it is a lot about yourself. How can a person write his own memoirs without referring to himself?

Well, I guess I'll let someone else figure that out. Maybe I could pretend I'm writing a novel and let the chips fall where they may.

Anyway, in my teenage years, it was expected that the law required kids go to school until you turned sixteen. The day you turned sixteen you could quit if you so choose. Most everyone did that since there was always a need on the farm for a husky sixteen-year-old boy or a sixteen-year-old girl for that matter. Therefore, most everyone quit school at the age of sixteen.

Now, the year that I was fifteen, with one more year to go, a man claimed that the government can't force a person to go to school until he turned sixteen. They only have to go to the age of fifteen. Well that caused a lot of stir in the Amish community. Most parents were willing to take advantage of the opportunity to keep their teenage children home to help on the farm.

My father and a few others didn't think it a very good idea to take advantage of someone's misprint or whatever reason they had to quit school when the intent of the law was to have them go until their sixteenth birthday. Therefore, my father sent me to school.

However, at New Year's, they opened up an old German schoolhouse for those that didn't go to the public school. Then my father took me out of public school and sent me to this German school.

There we learned to read and spell. Also, in the noon hour and a break in the forenoon and afternoon, we played simple games. It being wintertime, everything was done on the inside. The Farmer in the Dell was a favorite.

I'm assuming most everyone knows how that game is played. Therefore, I'm not going to explain it here, only to say that when your turn came to pick a partner, I always picked a certain girl, and that girl did the same. That was kind of the norm. In our case, we gave each other enough vibes to let us know that we have a connection without being too obvious to the rest of the players. These were our first interactions.

Nevertheless, about a year earlier, their school came to our school, and our school did likewise to their school to play softball. This same girl was keeping score. I tried to slip over to her a few times to check on scores and to see who was up to bat.

Then there came a time where we joined the young folks. I didn't join them until I was a few months short of my seventeenth birthday. She joined a few months later then I.

About that time, we were invited to my cousin's place on a weekend. I learned that she was also invited. Therefore, I took the courage to ask her if she desired to go with me. Having never been to such gatherings, let alone coming with a boy, put her in a shock with some hesitation. She declined.

At the time I was also shocked and not just a little confused. Nevertheless, I tried to take it in stride and hoped nobody would find out. As time went on, I still kept close track of her.

Now, in our community, we were allowed to have square dance parties in weekday events. Sunday gatherings were frowned upon for such activity.

In the process of these square dances, we learned that we were a perfect match. Whenever the opportunity arose, we would have a ball square-dancing. Somehow I mustered up enough nerve to ask her again for a formal companionship. This time she didn't decline. We had somewhat fellowship for close to a year. When we both decided it was time to become serious, I asked her for a steady companionship, which was the norm in our day.

Getting ready for a wedding—that was another matter we had to wait until everything lined up properly. I was in the Civil Service at the time and had off every two weeks on weekends and sometimes longer. In those days, it was accustomed to have weddings in the wintertime, mainly because of refrigeration of food. This took place on the seventeenth of January, and exactly one year later on January 17, we had our marriage ceremony performed.

As an understatement, I will say this year went by the slowest of any year of my memory. This sort of sums up a short version of my teenage years.

Unplanned rodeo

Breaking a New Horse

The first year that we were married I worked for my uncle in his welding and woodworking shop about a mile from where we lived on a farm that my father-in-law purchased for the purpose of work for his growing family.

Therefore, he asked me if I could keep on working for my uncle in his shop. Of course, I agreed that I would. We agreed to do the chores for rent, plus ¼ of the milk check for milking the cows. He furnished everything, except we furnished one half of the cows.

The chores included horses, 8 cows, 4 sows, 35 to 40 feeder pigs, and a small flock of chickens about 150 to 200 plus. In the spring we raised another five hundred extra pullets that we had on our own. I built my own brooder house and raised and sold the pullets in the fall. We also bought our own feed.

After the chores were done and breakfast was over, I was asked if I would ride and finish breaking a new horse that he had just purchased at the Shipshewana Auction. He told me, "This is the highest-strung horse that he ever had. He needs someone to ride him on a regular basis. Maybe if you rode him to work every day, he might simmer down a bit."

To say that this horse was high strung is a very mild phrase. Just looking at him told me he even looked like he could be some wild bronco. Just to get on his back was a challenge. He wanted to start running before a person could get halfway on his back.

It seemed like he could stand on four feet on the ground and jump straight up in midair and come down hard and do it again before a person could say, "Easy now."

Orpha would try to hold him and calm him down while I was struggling to get on him. As soon as I was on him, he would take off like a scared rabbit. I would ride him around in circles.

My wife grabbed my lunch bucket and held it out for me to grab it as he passed her. Sometimes it took a few circles until I got hold of it. He soon learned when I had the bucket, which was rattling, that it was time to head out to the long lane.

I don't know how fast he really went. All I knew was he or she—I guess she was a she because her name was Mable—only had one speed if you were able to get on her back, and that was fast. It was about a mile to my uncle's place, and she never slowed down, making a long turn at their driveway and galloping all the way to the barn door where she had to make a sudden stop. I always had to hang on to her mane to keep from flying over her head and heading head first against the barn door.

Going home was no different.

One morning, as I was getting ready to leave, buggies were coming from both directions. They all turned in at our neighbor's place that lived across the road from our driveway.

This neighbor lady had a quilting party. Therefore, all the traffic, which made Mable very nervous and extra hyper. She didn't slow down to make the corner turn. I was helpless in trying to slow her down. Reins in one hand, lunch in the other, you guessed the rest! She ran across the road through a shallow ditch, coming up out of the ditch and instantly stopping to keep from running into the fence too hard. I flew out over the top of her head, over the fence, and into the field.

Now, I was on one side of the fence, and Mable was on the other side and going down the road without me at full tilt.

Now the rest of the story was the women that watched the show, who laughed until they had tears.

The only thing that I lost was some pride and the time that it took me to climb back over the fence and walk the rest of the mile. When I got there, the horse was standing at the barn door, waiting for someone to let him in.

You can only imagine the laugh that the women had as she met me walking, and a minute earlier a horse whizzed past me at full gallop. She heartily waved a hand and had a broad smile on her lips as she passed me. I also forced a smile and kept walking.

I learned later that it produced some juicy gossip at the quilting party. Not every day do they get to see an unintended real rodeo act in real life.

Off to work

CHAPTER 11

Commitment for Life

Marriage

While attending a recent wedding, the first minister (speaker) spoke of the important event of the day. He proclaimed that we came together to fulfill the wish of two people that have been drawn together through love and decided they wanted to spend their lives together. He further stated that today was the day that two people would be made into one, and if the Lord tarried by noon today *we* would have made one person out of two. From then on, it would no longer be me, rather us.

This well-meaning minister meant it ever so well and had ever so good intentions. Yet what he failed to realize was that if *we* join these two together, where does that leave God? What will we make of God's work where he said, "What God had joined together, let not man put asunder"?

Man in the natural is not satisfied by taking God at his word, and on account of this one belief, he has to come up with a plan of his own. That is to have man set up in place of God and let man do the joining by the proclamation of some ritual and vows, thereby sealing two people together and making them into one.

The point I would like to make is, why not believe God's word and trust and believe in him that he is all that we need? A Godly joining will take place when two people, in a Godly fashion—thereby believing and trusting in his word—have committed themselves to the Lord and through him have been led to the understanding of his will. Knowing that the Lord has brought them together with that knowledge, they have drawn together through the love of God and for each other and want to spend the rest of their days together. Through that love of God and each other, they will become one when they physically join in the flesh. Now they have done what was ordained by God. The joining made them one, and hereafter they are no longer two, but one.

Now, there can be nothing wrong in having a wedding celebration, a time of rejoicing where two people have made a commitment to God and are planning to walk together as one in the Lord; a commitment that cannot be broken without great sin or death. This wedding celebration is nothing more than to let the public know that they have made a commitment. As they are rejoicing in their newfound love, they have invited friends, neighbors, and relatives to help them celebrate their joy in the Lord for his marvelous work and their newfound love.

God's Covenant in the Marriage Act

God's covenant in the act of marriage is no different or an exception from all of God's covenants, which the very act will be, or rather, is literally sealed with blood. This is the very fact in bringing a marriage literally, physically, and spiritually into complete oneness with God's purpose and his order, in complete union with God's order, him being the instigator and head, believing in God's word, through Christ, our savior, and the Holy Spirit. Here God's word is what God has joined together: let not man put asunder.

This is literally a true marriage performed by two people directed by God through Jesus Christ, through the Holy Spirit, and not by some ceremony by some man performing some manmade vows and joining in hands and pronouncing them, "Now you are no more two people but one. Husband and wife," thereby renouncing God's real order and purpose.

Now this is the rest of the story. I will have to admit that it is not an easy story to write.

First I'll have to explain how in our culture normally is considered a proper plan for getting married. The first move would be (in most cases) for the boy to ask the parents of a girl for permission to have communication for himself to or with the girl. Then if the parents consented and the girl agreed, they would then expect to visit with each other from time to time. Either or both visit together with her and the parents. They could also go places where other young folks would gather to sing and visit.

This could go on for several months or a year or more. Although long dating visits are discouraged, this is a very serious matter, and also much prayer and discernment are required or at least recommended.

Now, during that time, if they feel that God has made them to get married and become one spiritually and literally, they will ask the parents to plan for a time to make their commitment to become a reality.

In our case, Orpha and I did that. I had expected that would happen in a few months. That is when we would have the marriage ceremony to take place. However, in our case, it took exactly one year to the day when the ceremony and celebration took place. That was from the time we had made the commitment with each other to become life partners until the celebration took place.

Here I'll be bold and honest to say it was a long waiting game where my anticipated wife and I were in. Nevertheless, it taught patience, and in the end, it was all worth it.

To explain the folly of Apocrypha would take a small book. Yet I'll try to explain what I mean when a ceremony puts two people together to cause them to become one.

In our day, in their mind, it was considered the only proper way to join two people together. They went to the book of Apocrypha when, in the first place, it was only a history of how the people lived in captivity, not as spiritual teachings according to the New Testament. Also, people were searching for a marriage sermon and formula to use in proclaiming that now two people have become one. They could not find such a subject in the whole Bible for people to use to proclaim two people to become one by performing a ceremony. So they went to the Apocrypha. There they found what they were looking for. Now they found a way to justify the means of a wedding ceremony to join two people together.

But wait a minute, not so fast. The book of Tobias found in the Apocrypha has the writings of the people in the Babylonish captivity, found in the Catholic Bible as well as in the Lutheran translation of the Bible. I have one given to me at our wedding.

The writings were written in captivity when they were living in idolatry and witchcraft. It is meant for a history of that time and not teachings according to the word of God in the Old Testament.

Now, this is where the real test comes into play. We were upstairs in an unheated room. Outside was around fifteen degrees below zero and a strong wind blowing. A little more history. The wedding ceremony would take place in a different place than the reception. Ours took place in our folks' and dad-in-law's house, where we moved into a few days after the wedding.

It was always customary for the bride and groom to go to a separate room for instruction regarding our future of our married life. As in our case, it was at a father-in-law's house a quarter mile from each other, an upstairs room. Downstairs the congregation was singing slow hymns from the Ausbund for about an hour to an hour and a half while we were upstairs being taught the facts of life and getting colder by the minute. As fate would have it, it was January 17, and the temperature dipped to seventeen degrees below. When I woke up at 4:00 in the morning, my wife's brother and I stayed there overnight and kept the fire burning. Yet when I got up, the water in the tea kettle in the kitchen froze because the fire had gone out during the night.

At any rate, my brother-in-law and I did chores. I believe that everything that could possibly go wrong went wrong; including the water pump in the barn froze. At any rate, we finished the chores, thawed out the water pump in the barn, plus what seemed ninety-nine other things that we had to take care of. Nevertheless, we made it in time for the wedding. Thank God!

Now back to the upstairs room where six or seven ministers and my bride and I had assembled to be taught the facts of life. We were both wondering which would come first: they get finished with their rhetoric, or are we going to freeze first? About how long were we in the upstairs room, real time? About one hour; although it seemed like maybe four hours.

After we were sighing a breath of relief when the last one stopped speaking, just then the bishop thought of something he forgot to mention. This was it, and to say it lightly would be an utter understatement. He again brought up Tobias. This was not my father-in-law speaking (which was also his name). It was the Tobias in the Apocrypha. This was his statement.

Now, since his wife-to-be had seven husbands, and they all died the first night of their marriage, they had every reason to be skeptical of him becoming the eighth. Therefore, they waited three days or nights to come together. Also, for that reason, it is in our belief that couples should refrain from coming together for three nights as young Tobias did, which saved his life. This was the teaching we were taught in the upstairs room. This policy had been carried down through the years, including to and at the time of our marriage.

However, the bishop had almost forgot to mention something else. Maybe because it was so cold, or maybe he was tipped off by one of the others sitting close to him. Now, I hope this clears up the fact we were married by ceremony exactly one year after we promised each other to be committed to each other for life.

Now, this is the answer of what took place in the three days that we were told to stay apart. My wife and I were now being declared as no more "two of you"; rather from this moment on, we are no more two, rather one!

This statement was a proclamation made by a man. The big question now becomes, who should we believe? Whom should we put our trust in? The bishop proclamation, or the teaching of the Word of God in the Bible? When God proclaimed (in regards of two people becoming one) *which is this!* What *God* has put together, let *no man put asunder.*

To even make it clearer, why is God's statement not enough? What makes us want or think we should or have to include man in the matter? Why is *God's word not enough?*

Therefore, we also did what man is inclined to do—that is, to mix things up or maybe just not let things alone or as it is meant or taught.

In our case, since we were bluntly asked what we did during those three days of our *staying apart, what did we do?*

I'll try to cross all the t's and dot all the i's in telling what happened or what we made of this three-day waiting period.

First of all, Orpha and I had no time to discuss the matter. However, she did talk to her mother in passing. She told me that her mother informed her that they needed her bed for company and that I would have to sleep in the boy's room and she would sleep with the girls.

I told her that would be fine with me. I did not give it much thought since we were told to stay apart. I thought that would take care of the matter. I'll just enjoy the rest of the day, and that was now taken care of.

However, things have ways to change. Somehow the people learned that where they were going to sleep was Orpha's bed. When they learned that, they came to us and told us in *no* uncertain terms. This is what they said, "We learned this is your bed that was given to us to sleep in. Nevertheless, we are not doing such a thing! No way! Not for any reason *whatsoever* would we take your wedding-night bed from you. You two take that bed. Do not worry about us. We will find a place to sleep."

What this couple didn't know, which was this, they were from another state, and they apparently knew nothing of a three-day staying apart.

Later we went to her bedroom and had discussed nothing. Even now I was in turmoil since there was only one bed. What were we to do? I was too shy to ask her. She also didn't ask me. I decided to take my coat and vest off and slowly looked for a place to hang them up. Waiting to see what Orpha does, she was also hanging her dress up, leaving her undergarments on. I did likewise. There was nothing more to be said. Therefore, we went to bed.

Here is where I would like to stop and say, enough said. I was rather strongly advised to explain exactly what you had to go through on account of the three-day furlough.

For the first time, about twelve hours after the law was laid down, I asked Orpha what she thought of the part where we should stay apart for three nights. She said something like this, "I was too cold to really know what he was talking about. Whatever that was, it was their problem. Why was he so concerned about what we did?" she exclaimed.

It was her uncle that gave us the dictation. Since she held her uncle in high esteem, I thought she would embrace his teaching. In one sense I was relieved. Yet, on the other hand, I didn't feel like ignoring everything that he said since we were taught to honor our elders.

Therefore, I suggested a somewhat halfway decision. Why don't we just *not* go all the way for three nights, maybe just do a little testing?

However good that sounded, it was some of the worst advice or statement that I ever made up to that time.

Hindsight is twenty-twenty. What I did not take into account by the end of the third night is unexplainable. It would have been wise to tell Orpha, "This is your bed. You sleep in it. I'll sleep on the floor for three nights. That way, we will not go against your uncle's teaching," avoiding all frustration, guilt, and misery those three nights brought about. God forgive us for being so naive!

The three extra days were for what the bishop mentions as his last dictation for us. The good news is, I hear that this teaching has diminished or is very seldom mentioned anymore. Praise the Lord!

All the things, episodes, experiences, revelations, and many life happenings that took place in our lifetime in the last eighty-something years, which I have exposed in the writings, have been handed to a few others that I have known (most of them) for quite a number of years.

They were informed to not favor me but rather say it the way you think it shouldn't be written. That is to say, in Timothy 4–2 "reprove, rebuke, exhort, with all longsuffering and doctrine." That means, if necessary, rewrite, rephrase or do whatever is necessary to make it clearer or more meaningful.

Also, one especially wanted to be explained more in regards to where the wedding ceremony was being used to join two people together. The Bible is silent in regards for man to join two people by or with performing a ritual to make two people to become one. Therefore, some of our ancestors thought a couple should be joined together by somewhat of a ceremony.

They did find that in Tobias in the book of Tobias in the Apocrypha. This book was not written as a teaching of Christian principles or doctrine, only as a history of Judah in captivity in the land of Babylon.

There they lived in idolatry and witchcraft. Now to explain somewhat what happened and why the children of God were living in Babylon in the first place (my book is not intended to become a history book), I would encourage each individual to search those things out on their own.

Nevertheless, in as few words as I can, I'll quote what caused all this turmoil or idolatry and witchcraft. This is somewhat of a picture that I have in my mind by studying that history of those times. Basically, it all came about because of unbelief.

When Jesus came into the world in the form of a man and drew to himself a dozen humble fishermen and, should I say, misfits to follow him and drew many large crowds together and taught them about the kingdom of God, he taught them about the change of covenants from the old and into the new; also about many happenings that are going to take place and are at hand; as well as what it will take to bring all these things into reality, including his giving his life and the shedding his blood for a better sacrifice than the blood of animals; how the true worshipers will worship him in spirit and truth and not by performing or doing and act, like killing an animal and putting it on an altar in making or giving a sacrifice.

Thereby, he established a new order by setting the new order in their hearts and in their minds. No more doing or performing, *rather by being and believing. This being and believing comes from the kingdom of God by the Holy Spirit being becoming in us through the Holy Spirit and by our believing and trusting and becoming and following Christ through the cross and taking his yoke upon us and learning of him.*

In short, had the children of God followed this order and believed, they would not have found themselves in captivity still living in idolatry and witchcraft—all because of unbelief.

In summing this whole marriage ceremony up, why is it still used in proclaiming to having now joined two people together by making a proclamation, putting man in place where only God should be? While it is good that at least this three-day waiting game has played itself out after over two thousand years, why not also get rid of pronouncing two people being joined together by a man's statement and folly? And leave God's Word to do the commending!

Our Children's Book

I would like to lump you all together and give the same message to all. I so not esteem any one above another. You are all dear to my heart, yet in separate ways. I will start with the oldest, the firstborn.

You entered into my life when all was rosy. We were young and full of all the things that young people are full of. We had great expectations in life, and that was good. Things were going our way. We abounded with love for each other and dreamt of all the good things that were to come in our life. How we rejoiced and waited in anxious anticipation when we learned that we were to have one of God's miracles become a reality in our lives. When you would kick in your mother's womb, it was a joy to behold. Hid from us at the time, the thought of someday being able to claim you in real life and you being a part of us warmed and overjoyed our hearts.

However, one day all that changed. All our dreams came to a screeching halt; holding you in our arms and feeling you next to our beating hearts would never materialize. God saw fit to take you from your mother's womb. This, of course, we could never understand. Yet we have to accept it as God's proper choice. As much as we would have liked to have you with us in body, it was not meant to be. How your mother and I held each other in the hospital bed and softly wept together for you. In the same hospital room, there was another mother holding her newborn baby. It didn't seem fair that she had a bundle to take home, admire, and love, and we had to go home empty-handed. Physically your mother was worn out, but inside she was strong. She did not despair. How we wept over your limp body as we thought of not being able to have you with us even one day. God saw fit otherwise.

Now we know what God did to David, and we can understand and say with David, "We know you can't come to us, but we want to prepare ourselves to go to you." That longing has never changed. It has brought us closer to God. What a small sacrifice we have made in comparison to what he did for both of us. Because of that sacrifice, he had made it possible for us to come together again. We will then be able to rejoice and praise him together forevermore.

To this day and this very moment, when I think back to that hospital room when they brought your limp body in, how we admired you. Your mother was really drowsy and couldn't function very well, no matter how hard she tried. She did not cry as she held your limp body. She just adored it and talked about how nice you looked. Only when the nurse came to take you away did she break down. We softly wept together as the unfairness of it all began to sink in. The nurse knew we needed some privacy, so she pulled a curtain between us and the other mothers as we continued to weep for a long time together. Some tears of sorrow, yet I believe more were tears of joy. Even though at that time there was a lot that we didn't understand, we had faith and trusted that he had a purpose in all this.

Even though it was extremely hard to see any gain in this for us, we knew that all is for good to those who love the Lord. If it wouldn't be for this promise, which we believed, we would have very well despaired.

I will rehearse just a little bit here for the sake of memory and the other children. Not much was made of the funeral. It was at my mother's folks' place. My parents were present, along with my father's oldest sister and her husband, the Harley Smuckers, which were here. They were visiting from Ohio where they were living at the time, if memory serves me right. The only others present were your mother's parents and her brothers and sisters who were out of school. The ministers of the church were there also, but only the bishop, your mother's uncle Will, spoke. It was hard because your mother couldn't be there. She had to stay in the hospital. In those days you had to stay for a normal birth; your mother had to stay for three.

Here's a little more history for the ones that have an interest in how it came about. It was a Sunday. We spent the day with some friends who had invited us to a moon dinner, which was a normal custom. Your mother didn't feel well all day, and she sat on a hard chair the whole time. She was barely able to sit but didn't want to make a scene, so she just suffered the whole day through. When we came home, she laid down on the couch. I did the chores; at the time we milked seven or eight cows and cared for about two hundred chickens, hogs, and horses. When I came in, she was no better. Her brother, Elmer, and his girl-friend came to spend the evening with us. After they saw how ill she was, they soon left. I went to talk to your mother's folks about the situation, and they advised me to keep her calm, and all should be well.

When I came back, things were even worse. I quickly ran down the lane to our neighbor, Ivan Miller. After I called the hospital and described the situation, they advised me to bring her in right away. Ivan volunteered to take us. So we got in the back of his car and rushed back to the house. Though your mother was too sick to move, she got ready, and we left for town, six miles away.

They wheeled her into the labor room, and that was the last I saw of her for hours. That was undoubtedly the longest night of my life.

Soon after they took your mother in, Dr. Flannigan came marching down the hallway in his distinct stride that hardly anyone could copy. He marched right up to a washbasin in front of the labor and delivery-room door and proceeded to roll his sleeves up and lather his arms and hands. When he was thoroughly scrubbed and wiped, he slipped into the labor room where she was.

I breathed a sigh of relief, knowing a man was in charge that had lots of experience and knowledge. Nevertheless, at this point, things seemed to be getting progressively worse. At that point, I don't know what took place. I only know I heard your mother wince in extreme pain. This should have been a warn-ing to me not to put trust in man but in a higher power.

As time ever so slowly moved on, I was rapidly going from anxious moments to extraordinary hypertension, and I was on the verge of losing it all. I crept up close to the door where the nurses were ever so swiftly swooshing in and out with items of unfamiliarity. I tried to get their attention to ask about her condition, but their only reply was that I was supposed to stay in the waiting room; they would give me information soon enough. Even from where I was, I could hear her, and she seemed to be getting weaker and weaker.

At some point, the nurses changed shifts, and so I tried to get information on your mother's condition. Here I found a much-more-cooperative attitude. The nurse informed me that your mother was going to deliver, and she would be okay; however, the child would not live. The very thought that she was willing to share information with me was such a great relief. I could at least rest in the knowledge that my wife was going to be all right. Up to that point, I had no idea what was going on or what the outcome would be.

Later, when things quieted down, the nurse came into the waiting room and asked if I wanted to come in. Right then I just wanted to grab your mother and hold her, but I knew that would not be proper. So I just stood there and gazed at her in that fragile condition. She seemed to be in good spirits in spite of her groggy mind and was somewhat elated and glad I had come in. When she told me, "We're going to have a baby," all I could do was squeeze her hand and fight back the tears. Even though I didn't say a word, she seemed to cheer up some. I was thinking all the time the nurse had to be wrong, and I most certainly was not going to tell her what was going on.

I will never know exactly what took place. The only thing that the doctor said was the baby couldn't handle the delivery. I am only assuming that the baby passed out during delivery, and your mother was too exhausted to go on, so they quit and let her rest and catch her breath. Then they went in and pulled him out backward since they knew there was no life. It didn't matter how they delivered him. They just wanted to make sure your mother made it through. I think she had aftereffects that are with her up to this very day because of it. Today they would have had no second thoughts about doing a C-section, but it was almost unheard of back then. I don't suppose Dr. Flannigan had been taught or ever performed one.

In the meantime, we can only question what you are experiencing in paradise with Jesus. All the other children and your younger brother, we can only imagine the joy when you came together with your brother, telling him of all the wonderful things Jesus had done for you.

Again, I want to emphasize how much we wanted you to be with us and to share this precious time the Lord has given us here on the earth. Every day I am grateful to the Lord that I am part of his creation and that he had chosen me to be a piece of his divine plan. Nevertheless, I realize that Satan also has a plan and is here to cause as much trouble as he can. Therefore, we must keep ourselves in the presence of God and in the saving grace of our Lord and Savior, Jesus Christ, for only there can we find true safety. It is a great joy to be under his mercy and protection. Even though it is a vast place, we can find comfort and peace here in our Lord. Yet we still have to contend with Satan all the time. This part you have been spared from—Satan has no hold on you. Neither does he have any hold on us here, providing we keep ourselves in the shadow of the Lord. But Satan has many kinds of tricks. Unless we depend on our Lord and Savior for protection, he will trick us, and we will be no match for it. He has had more time than we can even count to prepare ways to deceive us into thinking that we are on the right track. But all the time we're following something he got out of his bag of tricks to make us believe we are following the Lord. Yet all the time we're following him.

I do not have to warn you about things, as I know you are safe in the arms of Jesus. Yet for us, here on the earth, this is very real. Again, our only protection is in Jesus—this we have to remind each other day and night. We must keep our eyes on him. Otherwise, Satan will come like a roaring lion, or maybe as an angel of light, and try to nab and deceive us.

This is what I need to write about to the ones that are still here with us. Starting with the next to the oldest, it was a great joy when we learned we were again experiencing a miracle of God. This time we rested in the Lord for whatever he had in store for us. As it turned out, we had a healthy little bundle. What a joy it was to hold you and watch you grow. I believe I was even more grateful for you because of what happened the first time. I believe we thanked the Lord not only every day but continuously for giving us a healthy child. As you grew, you brought us great joy. Those were once again happy years, and I recall many of them being because of you.

Supernatural Event

After a time of trials and testing, where we had lost our first son at childbirth, we were having a dream of maybe raising a family and living a life together in a church where everyone looked out for others and all looked to the Lord for all our needs and cares.

While we were having these testing, we also had our routine work to do. One of them was milking cows. One Sunday morning while we were milking, we (that is, my wife and I) were singing, which we did on a fairly routine basis. That morning we were singing a hymn entitled "Es Sin Schwanenweg in Dieser Zeit." There are two roads in these times. Now I will give some details of the setting.

The milk house was attached to the cow stable. There was a door that went directly into the milk house from the cow stable. This door opened into the cow stable from the milk house, and there was a screen door spring attached to the door to keep the door closed. This spring was attached in such a way that the spring laid against the flat door. Therefore, when the door was pulled open by a knob on the cow-stable side, the spring would screech and squeak as you opened the door.

Now, as we were singing this hymn, we noticed that this door was opening and closing all on its own, only that would be impossible. Therefore, I reasoned that my wife's brothers or sisters were playing a trick on us by somehow having attached a string to the door and were pulling on the string to open it and letting it go, and of course, the spring would close it. I knew that it would have to be them.

Therefore, I whispered to my wife, "I'll quickly go around the barn and surprise them." When I got there, to my surprise, there was no one around.

Now what? We debated if the spring made the noise as it normally did. Neither of us could recall a noise, yet we were not sure. Then we got our lantern and went outside and looked if anyone could possibly be around. It had snowed during the night, and there were only two sets of tracks around, which were made by my wife and I as we came from our house earlier. Now there was only one other possibility that door could open and close without a human being around, and that was that God had it open and close through the spirit. As we pondered the situation, it gave us an eerie feeling to say the least. We wondered what it meant, and what was God trying to tell us?

Although we believed in spirit and supernatural workings of God, we had never experienced a firsthand knowledge or an actual act of God in a profound way. Yet as simple as opening and closing a door. After this happened, it was hard for me to be in the barn by myself at night. What would I do if something like that happened again if I was all by myself?

However, as time went by, I became less self-conscious of the situation and didn't mind being in the barn by myself anymore. Then one Sunday morning I was milking by myself as my wife had our second child not too long before, and I was milking by myself. Unconsciously I was singing this same hymn again, and all of a sudden I realized that I was singing this song. I was milking the same cow in the same place in the stalls. I recalled what had happened a year earlier. I looked and peeked around behind the cow, and sure enough, that door was swinging wide open.

Hot chills went up or down my spine as I sat there, frozen, trying to think what to do. Then I got up and walked over to the door as it was swinging wide open and then shut again. I fully realized it did not make a sound even though the spring was scrapping the door. As I stood there, shaking in my shoes, I took ahold of the door and let my hand follow the door, not resisting as it swung back and forth. Then it stayed closed. So I took hold of the knob and opened it. I almost jumped out of shoes when it made its original screeching sound. Then I went to the house and told my wife what had happened again, and she understood.

It was hard for me to think about going out there again, and my wife wasn't able to go with me. My wife's parents lived down the lane about one fourth of a mile, so we decided to ask them if they could spare one of their children to come with me so I wouldn't be alone. When I told my dad-in-law what had happened, he just brushed it off and said, "It was probably just the wind."

Yet it was perfectly calm that morning, and nevertheless, if the wind had been blowing hard, that door would not have swung open steady without a sound. Anyhow, I went to church that day, and after church another young man that I knew very well was alone in the barn. So I told him about the incident that took place that morning. He also just brushed it off as some imagination and didn't care to hear about it. So this is what we decided to do—not tell anyone about it because it will only be believed as a hoax. Only many years later, after we had moved to Montana, did I muster enough nerve to tell our experience to a believer that did trucking for us. To my surprise, he believed every word of it. This gave me the courage to tell it to other people on a very limited basis.

This is now some fifty years later, and it is the first time that I put it on paper. The only reason that I am doing so is not to tell other people what an experience we had but rather that others might learn from it and bring them closer to God. Now for the meaning behind this, you may draw your own conclusion.

I still don't know just exactly what it all meant, yet I know that there is a spirit out there that does things that the human eye cannot see. I do know that Jesus is listening when we sing a beautiful hymn in his name and in his honor. This he did to my wife and I, to me twice and to my wife once, all in a simple thing by opening and closing a door without the touch of a human hand and without the wind blowing; all inside a building.

As we go through life, God shows us things all the time, and we are hardly aware of it. Yet when he does show us supernatural happenings as simple as opening and closing a door, this might shock us to reality that God, the maker of all things, always present, and we are oblivious of it. I do not believe we should dwell on experiences or consider strange happenings as a means of salvation.

Nevertheless, such things can draw us closer to God and in the process can affect the outcome of our life.

Life Happenings—The Shirt

I am now going to expose myself and tell you some of the happenings that took place in my lifetime not to draw attention to myself but only that others might benefit from it.

The first one that I should mention started when I was almost seventeen years old. It was customary that when a boy turned sixteen, his dad would give him a horse and buggy. I had two older brothers, and when they turned sixteen, they got their horse and buggy soon after that. When I turned sixteen, I had little desire to belong to the crowd of young folk with all the immorality and lack of spirituality that was going on. I realized that not all was bad, but a lot was not to be praised. Seeing all that, I didn't want to be a part of it. Therefore, I had little need for a horse and buggy. I guess my dad also realized that, and since I could also go with my brother that was two years older than I, there was no real need for another horse and buggy. Yet about two months before I turned seventeen, my dad got me a horse and buggy. Now I could come and go at my leisure.

As was customary, the boys in our area went to the country store on a Saturday evening. There we sat at the counter and drank cream soda and ate chocolate ice-cream sundaes. We listened to the Grand Ole Opry. Mom or Dad would always give us a little spending money anywhere from thirty-five cents to seventy-five cents and on a rare occasion a dollar bill.

One Saturday my mom gave me a five-dollar bill. I suppose this was for the times that I had stayed home and didn't get my allowance. She told me I could buy myself a shirt if I wanted to. I had planned to pick up my cousin, and together we were going to the country store. When he got on the buggy, I told him I'd like to go to town first and buy myself a shirt.

"So you want to buy a shirt. How did you get money for that?" he asked.

"Well," I told him, "my mom gave me $5.00 to buy a shirt."

"$5.00!" he exclaimed. "Just how do you rate? Nobody gets $5.00 from his mom!"

Well, I did and I was going to splurge! Now, since I went to a country school where we learned the three Rs, but speech was not stressed, we could converse in our Pennsylvania Dutch dialect, and nobody taught us to speak English. Therefore, my English left a lot to be desired. Now since I had all this money in my pocket, I felt like somebody.

So I walked right up to the clerk and said, "I want to buy a hem."

She apparently thought I said "ham" and advised me that I'm at the wrong place to buy a ham.

She said, "You should try the grocery store."

Then my buddy cousin quickly corrected me and told the clerk that I want to buy a shirt.

"Oh yes," I quickly exclaimed. "I want to buy a shirt!"

So she took me to the shirt department. I looked at the shirts and the prices. They didn't look all that dressy, and only fifty cents. I didn't intend to buy ten shirts. I only wanted to buy one shirt.

Then I asked her, "Do you have any other hems—I mean shirts?"

"Oh yes," she said. "We have others over there, but they are pretty expensive."

What she didn't know was that I had $5.00 in my pocket, and it was burning a hole in my pocket. So she took us over to these other shirts. Wow! They were nice! One was an aqua color and had two pockets with buttons on the pocket flaps, and was it nice. I said I'd take that one. It was $4.50.

Now I had a shirt and enough money left over to go to the country store, where I bought, to my shame, a pack of Camel (fifteen cents), a pack of gum (five cents), and a chocolate sundae for twenty cents; and I had a dime left for another time. I only wore this shirt on special occasions. Then there came a time when another person noticed the shirt and had a strong desire to have it. Since I had no intention of keeping everything for myself, I gladly shared. My former thoughts were of keeping everything as my own, therefore, I gave all that I had, and we shared equally. We now have been doing this for fifty-five years.

Now, over the years this shirt saw its better days and began to frazzle and wore at the cuffs and elbows. Yet there was still a lot left in the shirt. That was still good since it was made of good quality material. Back in those days the women didn't go to the store to buy their hygiene needs. They made do with what they had. Since this was good-quality material, she cut it into strips and made it into useful goods. Some were made for her own personal needs, and the balance went into carpet rags, where we used it to walk on or at the entrance to wipe our shoes before we walked on the floor.

Now I have written and explained how my self-righteousness, that was such a glowing presence, all turned out to become literal filthy rags.

Now, looking back, I can use this shirt as an example of how our spiritual self-righteousness will be like the shirt—no more than filthy rags that can be used for a time yet in time will be discarded in the same manner that the shirt was, thrown in the dump or the stove and be of no value.

CHAPTER 12

Teaching and Believing

My Upbringing

It is hard to decide what to write about next. I will touch a little on my upbringing. I grew up in LaGrange County, Indiana, in the largest Old Order communities. I married Orpha Yoder in January 1957 and had ten children. We lost our first son at birth in November 1957 and lost another son in 1974 in a farm accident at the age of eight. We raised four sons and four daughters. One son lives in Hillsboro, Wisconsin. One daughter lives in Minnesota, both Old Order; a daughter in Redding, California, in some denominal church. The remainder live here in the Libby community. A single daughter lost her husband from cancer.

We have from fifty to eighty people that come to our church here in Libby. Our doors are always open, and you and your family would be more than welcome to pay us a visit.

My wife is a cousin to Albert Mast and John Mast. I understand that John passed on.

We moved to Rexford in 1974. Therefore, we moved to Libby in 1992 and have lived here ever since and have no further plans. Even after all these years, we still strive and are getting closer to having a church as Paul writes about in 1 Corinthians 14:26–33.

Spiritual Awakening from a Storm

Spiritual Awakening from a Storm

Train up a child in the way he should go and when he is old, and he will not depart from it. This teaching should come in all sorts of ways, such as being an example and teaching them in all areas. I have no desire to mention all the ways that this teaching should come about, but I want to write about the teaching I received at nine years old in a totally unexpected way.

I only want to mention a case in point in my life. As far back as I can remember, we always went along with our parents to church. I'm not implying that everything was in proper order. Nevertheless, the services lasted about two and a half to three hours. We were required to sit through it and be attentive at all times. We learned from a young age that this was a place to be in complete reverence to the parents and the ones speaking as well.

This is just the way it was, and that fact was accepted without question. To this day I have more memories of what was said when I sat on the bench with my dad than of what was said several weeks ago or maybe even less than that. The point is the importance of being in submission in our younger years, how priceless and extremely valuable it is for children to grow up and being taught what is important in a man's life—living the virtues of a Christian character or the life of Christ.

This brings back memories of the early forties.

In the earlier years of our life almost all were farmers. Each family took their turn having a gathering for church, being that they all had barns and, of course, houses as well, but some of the houses were too small to seat all the people. Therefore, families with small houses had their turn in the summer and used their barns for service.

One Sunday, while we were attending services, this service was held in the thrashing floor of the barn. In the summer in the area where we lived we could expect a thunderstorm to come through the area about every two weeks. In the middle of the service, it got dark in the west. Everyone knew that a thunderstorm was in the making.

As we were growing up, we were always taught to go the house, as lightning was more apt to strike the barn than the house. Also, we were taught to not go to the water pump in the time of a thunderstorm.

In earlier years the farmers hauled their wheat and oat bundles to the barn and waited for the thrashing rig to come through to thrash the wheat and oats. In those years they used steam engines for power to run the thrashing machine. They would thrash until Thanksgiving or later.

The above is written to somewhat explain the history of our culture and how it was possible to have a group of people meet in a barn-thrashing den, and this is where this episode took place.

In the morning I had noticed that the preacher that had the main sermon that day was a minister from another district. Now, when he preached, everybody within earshot knew that someone was serious about preaching the Word in full force. In a normal sermon, this man could keep the audience spellbound. This was not a normal day. He not only had everybody spellbound, he had us literally shaking in our shoes. The harder it rained and the more the lightning flashed and the more the thunder cracked, the more earnest and louder he preached. No one was ever caught napping during his sermons.

While we were cooped up in this barn, lightning flashing and crackling, thunder bellowing and rumbling all around us, this man, driven by the Holy Spirit and by the power of God, was driving home to us the reality of heaven and hell, quoting scripture after scripture of getting right with God; that the time to do it is *now!* Today is the day to submit yourself to God!

As it started to get darker by the minute, the props that were put in place to push the bottom of the big barn doors out about four feet for ventilation were taken out. The big barn doors were closed. Even if we ran to the house, not all could fit in even if we all stood. Therefore, all we could do was to stay put and pray that God would spare us from being hit by lightning.

Then there were flashes of lightning, and a little later we could hear the rumbling of thunder in the distance. As the flashes got brighter and the thunder got louder, we knew it would start to rain soon. Then the rain came, and lightning flashed, and thunder cracked one after another.

Still this did not bother the preacher. As the lightning cracked and the thunder was all around us, he just preached louder and with even more intensity.

Then word came that the neighbor's barn was on fire. Most of the men went out to help with getting things out of the barn before it was too late. In the meantime, my dad stayed. He had four boys to stay with, plus a good number of other boys who were left with my dad to take care of them while they were helping with the burning barn.

These men dashed out into the pouring rain, hitched up the horse to the buggy, and went about one half of a mile down the road where the barn was burning. They saved the wagon and manure spreader and a small amount of wheat that was dumped on the ground by the buckets full.

Meanwhile, the service continued with only a few men left, a bunch of boys, and women and children. My dad and another man stayed and took the rest of the boys, except the younger ones who went to the mothers, as it was the custom for the men to sit on one side of the seating and the women on the other side.

This was the only church service that I ever attended that, as far as I can remember, everyone was not only in tears but

171

most were openly weeping, including the men and women that were left. The weeping was not about the thunder and lightning and rain but rather a brokenness and conviction of what was at stake with our souls. This minister had such a gift of bringing out the seriousness of life and how important it is to give our lives to Christ. The thunderstorm only helped him bring out the absolute importance of surrendering our lives to Christ.

The preacher was not so much preaching about fear of losing our lives. We all knew that was a real possibility. The emphasis was on being ready to face our Lord in the event that were to take place. That emphasis included the absolute importance of the word *today*, hammering home the words, "*Today if you will hear his voice, harden your hearts.*"

Therefore, today is the time. Today is the day of salvation! The intensity of the almost-constant thunder and lightning and the utmost sincerity of bringing forth the true word of God swept the ones in the barn off their feet.

I don't believe I was the only one that thought for sure the next strike would hit the barn we were in. However, that was not the case. Nevertheless, the point is that, had we not been accustomed to going along to church, we would never have had the experience of this wonderful episode—at the time very alarming yet in the end an everlasting experience to be treasured for life.

Here, again, the weeping did not come from fear of losing our lives by being struck by lightning, only much more of being filled with the fear of God and reckoning with our Lord. At that time, being nine years old, I gave my life to the Lord, asking Him to receive my spirit as it was proclaimed by the one that spoke.

I am certain that I wasn't the only one that promised God if he would see us through that we would forever be grateful to him and follow him whatever might befall us or come our way.

God's presence was so close, and our obedience to him was so sincere to this day I have not forgotten my desire, and neither had he.

To this day I am thankful to the Lord and the impact this had on my life. He brought this minister and the thunderstorm together, teaching and showing us his mighty power; realizing how frail and weak we are, and all that we can do is lift our thoughts to him and plead for mercy because we are always at his mercy. Now if we believe that and fully trust in him that he will never leave us nor forsake us, then there is no need to fear, and the time to make yourself right with the Lord is now. Do not wait until a crisis happens because then it is too late. Even at nine years old, and as frightened as I was, this message brought by this sermon was received clearly and remains with me still today.

Believing and Not Believing

I would like to write a subject on believing and not believing. I'll try to keep it short and to the point. Yet it might take a little explaining to get the message across.

Let us start with Phil. 3:2–18. Paul warns us of what and of whom to be aware of. He says beware of dogs, beware of evil workers, beware of the concision.

In the Old Testament, only the shed blood of the offering of the Lord, which points to the shed blood of Christ upon the cross, was acceptable unto the Lord. Therefore, when the prophets of Baal "cut themselves" until the blood gushed out upon them, the people of God knew that this was a direct violation of the law of God. Yet they could not decide who was Lord of all. They had been seduced by that woman, Jezebel. Jezebel was a false prophetess, a message of Satan. (Rev. 2:20) Therefore, in the days of Elijah, Satan, out of his evil depths, was bringing forth a message and a messenger that he would use against his people of God until his final destruction in the lake of fire. This was the message of the false cross.

The following is a clear message that includes us right along with the people of Philippi. Paul calls the false messenger dogs and evildoers. Then he tells us what they do that we have to be aware of them.

Listen to their message, it is a watered-down message of concision. The word concision means to cut up or cut off or mutilate. That is exactly what we hear of those smooth-talking people, like the ones that Jesus was talking to where he called them for what they were doing. This is what he said, "You travel land and sea to make one proselyte and when he is made you make him two fold more the child of hell then yourself." (Matt. 2:3–15) Now, in Phil. 1–29 it says this, "For unto you is given on behalf of Christ. *Not only to believe in Him, but also to suffer for His sake.*" These are not my words; therefore, I can only suggest that we ponder on those words.

Reconnecting the Generations

Pride and preferences have kept the generations from reconciling with one another. The thing that has kept the generations from reconnecting and walking together is pride and preferences on both parts. When we make our own preferences, or our own opinions, into a law or a tradition, it can become legalism and allow a religious spirit to corrupt our love for one another. The Father of lights wants to restore the generations to one another. It will take both parts being willing to lay down their own pride and preferences in favor of relationship with one another. We must accept that our sons will go places with the Lord where we have never been.

The gospels Mathew, Mark, and Luke all make note of Jesus exhorting us all to remain new wineskins. We are in the beginnings of a great revival and great awakening, but only those that remain fresh new wineskins toward the Lord and one another will be able to receive and participate in this anointing.

I was told this letter was intended for only me. Nevertheless, it was also sent to the congregation in Libby, as well as the congregation in Indiana. Therefore, I also will send them this answer:

> Greetings in the name of Jesus. Grace be unto you and peace from him which was and which is to come. Revelations 1–4 In acknowledgement to your letter, I want to thank you for writing me and asking me in a phone call if it is all right to send it to me.

Now I have a responsibility to acknowledge the same. The only thing that I will say is this. In the first statement regarding reconciliation, if we have been reconciled to Christ and are following him—having denied self, taken up our cross, and are following him (Mark 8–34), also have come unto him (Matthew 11–28) on our own, we have no defense and are completely defeated. We are totally dependent on him. He is our rock; on him we stand by taking his yoke upon us. We learn to pull with him instead of for him, that he is meek and loving in heart, and we shall find rest for our souls.

Therefore, there is no room for pride and preference. It has been nailed to the cross and washed in his blood.

I realize this is the answer to your first statement. Nevertheless, the other statements would have the same answer. Therefore, *I rest my case.*

We have come to the end of our journey for now. Therefore, my hope is that these life stories of happiness, fun times, hardships and sufferings have demonstrated the purpose of this book.

In life, we all have ups and downs but when we learn of Jesus and deny self by putting our faith in him, he will always be there to assist us in overcoming anything that life throws our way. These circumstances are demonstrated throughout these stories. He is always with us to lighten the load even during the most extreme situations. Which allows us to experience the needed rest for our souls.

ABOUT THE AUTHOR

Ora and Orpha Miller when they were on a trip to Hawaii in 2013.

Ora Miller was born in Northern Indiana and grew up in one of the largest old-order Amish communities. He attended school until the eighth grade. Ora loved history and school but did not go to college or got a degree. In the Amish culture it is common for children to leave school at a young age to help their folks with farming.

Ora's family moved from Indiana to a small Amish community in Rexford, Montana. They were the fourth Amish family to live in Rexford. Then the family bought 830 acres in the country, ten miles southeast of Libby, Montana.

Ora married his beloved wife, Orpha (Yoder) Miller, in January 1957. They have enjoyed sixty-three years together to date. The couple had ten children but suffered the loss of their first son due to a buggy accident, causing him to be born too early in November 1957. They lost another son at eight years old in a farm accident in 1974.

Ora and his family live on the property outside of Libby in a small community. Five of their children reside on the same property. Three of their children live elsewhere. Ora's entire family has been raised and taught in the Amish culture and continue to give praise to God for the blessings he has bestowed upon them.

CPSIA information can be obtained
at www.ICGtesting.com
Printed in the USA
BVHW081210050820
585525BV00002B/5